ARCTIC ADVENTURER

by

Rob Ellis

Highgate of Beverley

Highgate Publications (Beverley) Limited
2012

Acknowledgements

My grateful thanks are due to the following: Front cover – Dennis Chapman; Graphics –
Skipper Ken Knox; Photos – John Crobbelar.

British Library Cataloguing in Publication Data.
A catalogue record for this book is available from the British Library.

ISBN 9781 902645 58 2

Published by
Highgate of Beverley

Highgate Publications (Beverley) Limited
24 Wylies Road, Beverley, HU17 7AP
Telephone (01482) 866826

Produced by
Highgate Print Limited
24 Wylies Road, Beverley, HU17 7AP
Telephone (01482) 866826

PROLOGUE

Fishing in the Arctic in the late 1950s and early 1960s was not as prolific as it had been in the years immediately after the war, forcing skippers and their crews to be more alert and focused than ever. Up-and-coming officers like Bob had to try and learn from each skipper they sailed with in order to make an instant impact whenever the chance came to take a ship. The object was to learn as much as possible about the fishing grounds by staying with the top skippers in the top ships, and so achieve recognition. This is the story of how – despite physical handicap and pressure of expectation – one young hopeful pursued this path to the top.

NOTE

One fathom = six feet

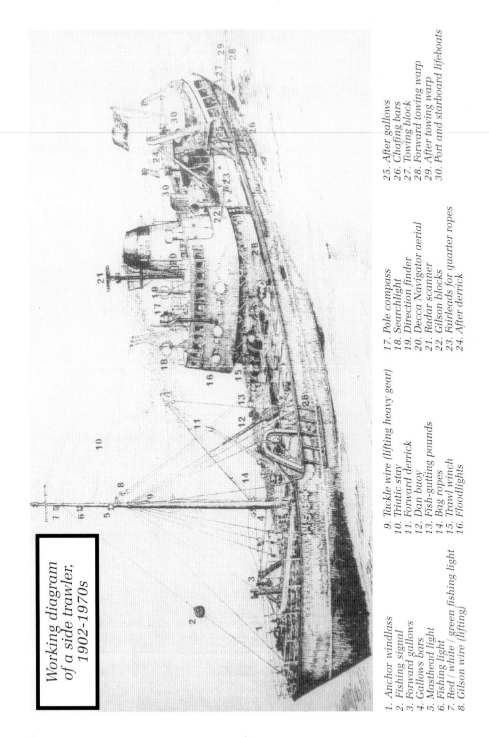

Working diagram of a side trawler, 1902-1970s

1. Anchor windlass
2. Fishing signal
3. Forward gallows
4. Gallows bars
5. Masthead light
6. Fishing light
7. Red / white / green fishing light
8. Gilson wire (lifting)

9. Tackle wire (lifting heavy gear)
10. Triatic stay
11. Forward derrick
12. Dan buoy
13. Fish-gutting pounds
14. Bag ropes
15. Trawl winch
16. Floodlights

17. Pole compass
18. Searchlight
19. Direction finder
20. Decca Navigator aerial
21. Radar scanner
22. Gilson blocks
23. Fairleads for quarter ropes
24. After derrick

25. After gallows
26. Chafing bars
27. Towing block
28. Forward towing warp
29. After towing warp
30. Port and starboard lifeboats

CONTENTS

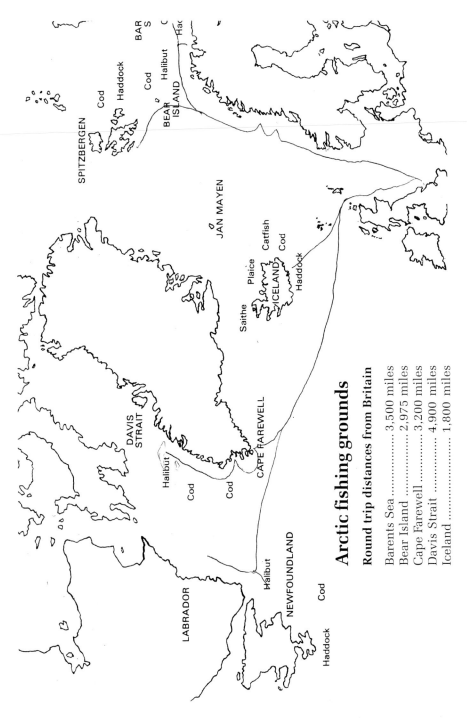

Arctic fishing grounds

Round trip distances from Britain

SPITZBERGEN

Cod

Haddock

BAR
S

Halibut

Cod

Halibut

BEAR
ISLAND

Ha

JAN MAYEN

Catfish

Plaice

Cod

Saithe

ICELAND

Haddock

DAVIS
STRAIT

Halibut

Cod

CAPE FAREWELL

Cod

LABRADOR

Halibut

NEWFOUNDLAND

Cod

Haddock

Barents Sea .... 3,500 miles
Bear Island .... 2,975 miles
Cape Farewell .... 3,200 miles
Davis Strait .... 4,900 miles
Iceland .... 1,800 miles

CHAPTER 1

THE NEW CHALLENGE

I had seen many trawlers in my short life and I knew this was no mere fishing-boat now overtaking us as I watched through the wheelhouse windows. But it was certainly out to catch something and it soon became the focus of a very exciting scene. Not very large, perhaps a little more than tug size, the ship had a long fore-deck and a squat stern. It was certainly capable of ice-breaking – the severe rake of its sharp stem told me that. But there were two real give-aways: the gun-like fitting mounted on the end of the catwalk running from the wheelhouse to the fo'c'sle head; and the barrel-shaped structure near the top of the large foremast, the so-called crow's nest for a look-out. This was a purpose-built whale-catcher, and as we steamed north in the Norwegian Sea that's exactly what she was doing.

I watched in anticipation as the little ship sped zigzagging past us in pursuit of a pod of four whales. Head and shoulders peeping out above the rim of the crow's nest, a man was indicating the direction of the nearest sounding whale, pointing down first over one bow, then the other. Those on the bridge were struggling to follow his lead and get close enough for a shot from the harpoon-gun on the bow as soon as the whale next surfaced for breath. It was fascinating to watch.

I was on my first trip as bosun on a modern deep-sea trawler bound for the Arctic fishing grounds, and you couldn't get much more modern than the *St Loman* in this year of 1957. At that time she was probably the largest side-trawler ever to sail out of Hull. As bosun I was second officer in charge of the deck, and also of this early-evening watch on the bridge. With me were two other watch-keepers, Jim and Ron, both currently employed as look-outs. We had no need of a helmsman on this modern ship with its automatic pilot.

I suppose twenty-one is pretty young to get a start as bosun on a ship like the *Loman*. What's more, I was newly returned to sea after a serious operation that had cost me half a lung, and it had been tough to persuade those who sanctioned my certificates – the doctors and the owner's insurers – that I was fit enough to do the job. But Johnny Dowsam had shown no hesitation in promoting me: I'd sailed with him many times before and he'd been impressed by my performance since my return.

I've always had a lot of respect for Johnny Dowsam. He was a quiet, no-nonsense type with a steely determination to succeed, even if appearances might suggest otherwise. Short and chubby-faced, overweight from his years on the bridge, Johnny had long since lost all his teeth. Like most fishermen, he didn't wear his false set at sea lest he lose them, so any sharp response he made was a gummy one, highly unlikely to instil terror. And he routinely wore downtrodden carpet slippers – hardly suitable footwear for someone constantly up and down accommodation ladders.

However, Johnny's amiable disposition could be misleading. He refused to stand for any insubordination or over-familiarity, as many a decky soon learned to his cost. Very few people knew the skipper's full story. He had been toughened up as a merchant seaman during the war, when his ship was shelled and sunk by the German battleship *Admiral Graf Spee*. He was captured and imprisoned in the *Altmark*, the notorious German prison ship, and then – more traumatically still – bombarded by the British when the navy came to the rescue.

My two watch-mates were discussing our new ship and its skipper. 'What's this bloke like to sail with then, Bob?' asked Ron. 'They reckon his nickname is John the Baptist. Is that because he's a stormy bastard who'll baptise us all in salt water?'

'What do you expect with a name like Douse 'em,' I quipped, my binoculars still trained on the whale-catcher.

'I've sailed with him before,' said Jim, a clean-cut, roly-poly thirty-year old. 'He's firm but fair. Mind you, he does push it a bit at times.'

'With a ship this size to fill, I think you'll find him pushing it most of the time now,' I replied.

While the lads continued to discuss the stormiest skippers they'd sailed with, I spotted a man running down the catwalk to the bow of the whale-catcher. Grabbing the harpoon-gun, he quickly took aim and fired a shot into a whale surfacing just ahead of him. The catcher was just too far away for the boys to see this kind of detail, but I was transfixed by it all. The hefty harpoon pierced the whale; then came what seemed like a further explosion, followed by a spurt of blood. A couple of thrashes and the beast stopped literally dead in its tracks.

Why run all the way down the catwalk from the wheelhouse? I wondered. Surely the man firing the gun could have stayed in position on the fo'c'sle head. Was the captain trying to control as much of the hunt as he could? Or, and perhaps more likely, did a crewman risk getting stuck out there during the chase in danger from the pounding seas?

'Surely the weather won't bother us too much in a big ship like this?' Ron was saying. At nineteen, he was still a bit naive where deep-sea fishing was concerned. Thin and wiry, he had recently got his girlfriend into trouble and was sticking with the job to earn some money to get married.

'Don't you believe it,' I replied, still intent on the scene ahead of us. 'When there's a big ship to fill, most skippers will keep on fishing when they should be pulling back. And the bigger the ship, the heavier the water it takes on in bad weather.'

The whaler hove the stricken leviathan alongside with the harpoon-line, and some sort of flexible pipe went over the side and into, or close to, the wound. A short while later the crew removed the pipe and attached a floating buoy to the whale before casting it adrift. What were they doing? I wondered. Had they pumped air into the carcass? Whatever they were up to, it enabled the vessel to continue chasing after the remaining whales, who to my surprise had stayed in the area. The speedy little vessel eventually moved off in a different direction, presenting its stern to me and so blocking my view of any further action. I'd clearly witnessed something extraordinary. Very few fishermen, let alone land-lubbers, would experience that in a lifetime. No doubt there'd be a factory ship somewhere close by.

I turned away to concentrate on my duties. Glancing at the radar, I flicked through the ranges to check for other ships in the vicinity. Next a quick look at the sal log gave me the speed and distance run since the last setting. And finally, with a word to my watch-mates to warn me if the catcher returned, I stepped into the chart-room to fill in the log-book.

As a fresh-faced young bosun, I was acutely conscious of my position. I was under scrutiny, not only from the skipper and mate, but also from the rest of the deck crew. Twenty men might depend for their lives on my competence and alertness, and the responsibility always struck me most forcefully during watches like this. I also knew how important it was to display confidence and determination, especially when I was in charge of the deck. Always in the thick of it – particularly during hauling and shooting when speed is of the essence – the man who controls the deck works hardest of all. He has to keep an eye on everything and everyone. He's in the waist of the ship, its most vulnerable area, as the gear comes in. And when the catch appears, he's on the fore-deck, releasing the cod-ends and getting swamped by fish.

The log now complete, I entered our position on the chart, less out of duty and more for my own satisfaction. We certainly wouldn't be making landfall on the Lofoten Islands this watch. Returning to the bridge, I found the two lads still chit-chatting, the last of the daylight fading in the west. Suddenly we realised the old man had shuffled into the wheelhouse. Startled, Ron blurted out a cheery greeting. 'Now then, Skipper. How are things going?'

Johnny considered his reply for some time. 'You're the one on watch,' he said slowly. 'You should be telling me – if and when you're asked, that is.' Then, as if to emphasise the point, he turned to me. 'Everything all right, Bob? Any traffic around?'

'Not a lot,' I replied. 'That guy far off the starboard bow is a whale-catcher, moving away from us now. And a Russian timber boat passed us going south. That's the only other vessel I've seen. He's way over on the port side. On his way to Hull, I bet.'

'More than likely,' said the skipper. Hull was after all the largest timber port in the UK. 'I'm just off to check out the reports with the sparks. Then I'm going for a lie-down till the next watch comes on.'

'Aye aye, Skipper,' I replied.

'Excuse me, Skipper!' Jim butted in. 'Is it all right if we have a bit of music on the bridge?'

'All right with me, if the bosun's happy with it,' drawled Dowsy, one eye on me.

Taken aback, I paused for a few seconds. I'd have to get used to being consulted like this. 'Fine with me. I don't think it'll distract us.'

'OK, you can have it on till the wireless operator goes below. Then he'll have to tune you into 2182kcs. You can listen out on the calling frequency.' And with that Dowsy stepped off the bridge and into the wireless room. Soon the bridge speaker crackled as the sparks whizzed through the stations, shortly followed by Radio Luxembourg playing tunes from the Top Twenty. The boys settled down to listen, arms on the window-sills and foreheads against the glass, staring out at the horizon.

I too was lounging against a window, watching the red glow of the setting sun as 'Ghost Riders in the Sky' droned across the bridge. I gazed down on the huge fore-deck, with its high bulwarks and larger than usual hatches, fixtures and fittings. Lucky I'm so tall, I thought. It'll certainly make it easier to negotiate these higher working parts. Still, I'll have to bear it in mind when I hand out jobs to the smaller lads. Mind you, I knew sorting that out would be the mate's job to start with.

We had put the trawl alongside ready for use but there was still plenty to do around the deck before we could shoot. Another twenty-four hours would see us well inside the Arctic Circle, right in the middle of the fishing grounds, where Dowsy would select our starting-point. Over a quarter of the way into the year, we were probably too late to fish the west coast of Norway, the closest grounds in this area. And a good job too, I reckoned. These were among the most difficult grounds of all. You had to drag the trawl along the sides of underwater mountains, and the strong tide at your back meant that you could only tow one way. In consequence you had to steam back and scramble the gear aboard nearly every haul, putting the deck officers under even greater pressure than usual.

The adjoining grounds off the North Cape looked more likely. But Dowsy might also decide to carry on even further north and head for Bear Island. The next thirty-six hours would tell.

Over the following day, the Arctic weather started to show itself. I was in charge of the deck in the morning as lowering cloud moving down from the north turned everything greyer and greyer. A fresh Force Five blowing from the NNW swept down from East Greenland. Although not enough to drive us off deck, its bite was still harsh and made our lives pretty uncomfortable. The seas continually smacked the port bow and sheets of icy spray soaked us through, stinging our eyes and faces with salt. I knew the men around me were pretty pissed off, and that I was the focus of their discontent. Surely we could be doing something different under the fo'c'sle head? Or down below in the hold or the fish-room?

But we still had jobs to complete before we could shoot the gear. And I'd be the one feeling the wrath of the skipper and the mate if I did the easier tasks now and we couldn't get back on deck because the weather worsened. Making unpopular decisions like this was the first test facing any officer.

Only half the crew was with me on deck, just my watch (minus one look-out) and the daymen, five of us in all. The traditional leader of the daymen is the fish-room man, the crewman who takes charge of work in the fish-hold when the mate is unavailable, in this case one Barry Pike. An angular man of above average height, Barry was hollow of cheek and bony of face. He was very hard working and knew it, and as such was a favourite with the mate. For obvious reasons, he was at the forefront of most of the complaints.

First we had to shackle up the thirty fathoms of cables connecting the towing warps to the actual trawl. We laid the cables along the deck, shackle up, as far as the mouth of the trawl, fore and aft, before winding the rest on to the winch. Next we laced some extra floats to the top edge of the trawl, and then continued with other odd jobs as we raced along, bouncing from one wave top to another. Glancing outboard from time to time to check on the weather, I spotted a few trawlers about, all towing north in a ragged line. It looked like we'd arrived on one of the west coast banks. Might there still be some fish here for us even though the season was just about over?

The skipper was on the bridge, banging the windows up and down, keenly interested in these ships and their activities. A dozen or so were following the edge of the bank, nothing like the hordes you'd get in mid- season. The old man would certainly be calling up any skippers he knew to glean more information. Pretty soon we passed a foreign ship stopped in the water hauling. Even I could see his trawl laid out on the surface with a load of fish in it. This'll be it, I thought to myself. It looks too good for Dowsy to resist.

Sure enough down went a window and out came the dark, tousled head. 'Call 'em out,' Johnny shouted, his voice calm but firm.

Call 'em out. Hell, we were barely ready! We still had things to finish off, among them putting the cowhides on the cod-ends to stop them chafing out on the sea-bed – a job reserved for the mate. Everything had to be done by the time the old man got the ship into position.

'Fucking hell!' snarled Barry, throwing down his spanner. 'I knew this would happen. I'm going down the fish-room to ice the bottoms ready.'

'No, you're not,' I overruled him. 'You'll have plenty of time for that once we've shot the gear. Help me spread these cod-ends out ready for the mate.'

'Snacker!' I shouted to the decky learner. 'You run and call 'em out, but cut through amidships and call the mate first.'

Barry carried on moaning – preparing the fish-room was his responsibility, after all. 'The mate won't be happy,' he whined.

But I knew what would worry the mate more. Finding fish so unexpectedly hadn't just caught out the deck crew. The skipper must have hinted to the mate that we'd probably carry on further north, otherwise they'd both have been pushing much harder. From that moment on, we were constantly running to catch ourselves up. After a short delay we finally got the gear down but a short tow left us still trying to organise the deck when a bellyful of fish shot to the surface.

Of course, we had to deal with this first – gutting it, washing it and putting it down below. The fish-room men were unprepared for a catch of this size and needed extra help, so we couldn't get clear before we were hauling again. And so it went on – Dowsy piling up the deck and us playing catch-up. The weather did nothing to help our cause either. The wind had backed to the SW and we were now bashing into it at full speed when we steamed back every other haul.

Standing waist deep in fish, muffled up, sou'wester on, and swept by heavy spray, I reminded my watch-mate Jim of my earlier comments. Dowsy just had to go in hard: he was new to this command and would want to repay the owners' confidence. And any man skippering a ship the size of the *St Loman* would want to prove himself better than the rest, even if that meant pushing himself and his crew to the limit and beyond. It was tough on me coming back to this kind of scenario after two years off sick. But I'd said I could do it, and do it I must.

My new job as bosun certainly made more physical demands than that of the decky, especially when I had control of the deck. But even when the mate was in charge I still had one of the otter-boards to work. Weighing up to a ton or so, the two otter-boards (or after doors) lie on either side of the mouth of the trawl, serving to kite or hydroplane it open. Leaning over the side to chain them up when they come spinning out of the water is one of the most dangerous positions on deck, especially in bad weather when the ship is continually taking on water. And working the board at the after end – always more susceptible to taking the seas aboard as the deck and rail are closer to the water – is usually the more difficult and dangerous.

Each time we steamed back we should have been lifting the boards clear before proceeding on at full speed. But Johnny Dowsy was in no mood to wait. He was ringing the telegraph as soon as the fish was on board, so the door was scooping up water even before we'd got the lifting hook of the Gilson wire into the ringbolt, let alone secured the wing of the trawl to stop it washing outboard. When a ship as powerful as the *St Loman* is steaming full speed with heavy weather on the bow, she often dips her rail, chopping the tops off the oncoming seas and sweeping tens of tonnes of water along the deck. Whenever this happened the three of us had to leap up, grab the safety-rail on top of the engine-room casing and scramble up the side – hopefully in time to avoid the crashing, surging water beneath us.

If you're too slow and the seas catch you, your only option is to cling tight to anything high enough, trying at all costs to avoid the angry water ready to drag you along the deck and bash you against all the obstructions and fittings that line it. Ringing the ship up full speed before anything was secure was a very dangerous practice. But health and safety had absolutely no say in this job – time was money and the skipper's word was law.

The next few days were a harsh struggle, icy squalls hitting us periodically as the weather failed to improve. Dowsy really had the bit between his teeth now and was pushing things as hard as he could before the fish took off, inevitable so late in the season. Tempers were beginning to fray, the crew snarling and moaning when the skipper couldn't hear them. The mate, of course, should have nipped this in the bud. But that was not Ben Smith's way.

Bald, square-shouldered and ruddy-faced, Ben was very experienced and in many ways a good mate. However, his lack of drive and the will to push on seemed to have cost him all chance of promotion. Nor could he keep a solid grip on the crew. The skipper made up for this to some extent; but Dowsy couldn't have eyes and ears everywhere.

As we were fishing mainly in daylight hours, steaming back during the day would cost us one good haul. But Dowsy had a plan – towing all the way up the bank, then steaming all the way back through the night. This seemed to pay off at first, with reasonable hauls each time. But the weather continued to deteriorate as the days went by. It wasn't so bad while we were towing with the weather behind us, but each time we steamed back we bashed into it again and again, scooping up some heavy seas over the fo'c'sle head.

Since some of this heavy water was falling among the fish and threatening to wash it away, the old man was forced to ease the ship in to half speed while the catch was on deck. You could sense his impatience as he continually stepped up to the windows and peered out through the flying spray to see how we were doing. Better if the *Loman* wasn't moving so violently, was the answer. We were still moving along at a fair lick.

With most of the fish in the hold, the skipper called Ben up to the bridge, wanting the mate to relieve him while he caught some much-needed rest. Ben grabbed my arm as he passed by, shouting in my ear above the roar of wind and sea. 'When the fish is clear you need to stretch out the cod-ends before you lash them up. There are some hides hanging off.'

I grimaced and nodded, glancing round at the water landing on the fore-deck. Fixing the hides was the mate's job, but Ben had been short of time when we first stopped to shoot. Now we'd have to spread the cod-ends right out on deck and reattach the hides with strips of nylon twine known as seizings. The skipper gave the mate his orders. Then, with the last few fish sliding down into the fish-room, he rang the ship on full speed and left the bridge.

The chief engineer now opened up the stop-valve, increasing to near maximum the thrust of probably the largest steam-engine ever put into a trawler, and sending the *St Loman* rushing into, rather than over, the oncoming seas. With the ship rolling, lurching and pounding into the waves, the half dozen men around me struggled and staggered in their attempts to spread the heavy, double-twined cod-ends out flat. Spume filled the air, and the heavy water scooped up by the bow came pouring down from the fo'c'sle head to the fore-deck, washing men and net towards the waist of the ship with barely a seizing fitted. Even by the risky standards of fishermen, it was very dangerous to be working on the fore-deck while steaming full in this weather, especially in such a powerful ship.

I tried to spread out the nets by putting two Gilson wires in the corners of the cod-ends and heaving on the winch – but without success. Each time we lowered a net to the deck, another sea would follow two minutes later and wash us all towards the after end of the fore-deck. Five times we tried it, with help from the two fish-room men for our last three efforts, but still we couldn't finish the seizings.

'I've had enough,' said Barry Pike at last. 'I'm not trying again unless the ship's eased in.'

The others agreed.

'Well, the mate's up there now,' I retorted. 'He's your buddy. Why don't you go and tell him?'

'Not me!' snorted Barry. 'I'm off to empty the water from my boots. You go on up.'

Off he staggered along the deck to the drying-room on the casing top above the engine room. And, ignoring my protests, the others followed suit – heads down, salt spray streaming from their faces. I saw no alternative but to follow them, glancing up at the bridge windows as I did so. Was that Ben's face I saw framed for a moment beyond the floodlights? He must have been aware of our plight. Grimly, I climbed the steel-runged ladder and entered the drying-room surrounding the funnel. The men were all inside, sorting themselves out and readjusting their waterproofs, and I took the opportunity to empty my thigh-boots, by now full up to the knees.

As I tipped out the water, Barry spoke up. 'You're not the only one can do that, you know,' he said guiltily, wiping his face with his muffler.

'I know what you can do,' I snapped. 'What I'm finding out is what you can't. You've had a chance to catch your breath. Now we need to get out there and finish the job.' I had to try and persuade them to go out again, but in my heart of hearts I knew it wasn't on.

'It's no good, Bob,' one of the other lads chipped in. 'We've tried hard enough. We just can't do it unless the mate eases her in a bit. Can't you go and have a word with him?'

'OK,' I said. 'But it won't be for long, so be ready to drop down on deck straight away. We'll use the Gilsons again.'

Leaving the warmth of the drying-room, I squelched up the ladder to the bridge veranda in my sodden boots. When would I ever get the chance to dry them out? Ben was switching his attention from compass to radar to echo-sounder, the bridge shaking each time the bow pounded into the seas, spray streaming down the windows. He looked up anxiously as I came in. 'Is the job done?' he said. 'Have you managed it?'

'I think you know the answer' I replied. 'You must've seen what a struggle we've had. The lads are soaked and exhausted. We need you to ease her in for a little while just to get a few more seizings on.'

'I can't do that.' Ben was concentrating hard on radar and sounder. 'We're already struggling to get back to our starting-point in time. You'll just have to persevere.'

'We have persevered. Time after time. And the truth is the lads won't turn to until the ship's eased down. Just ease her back for a few minutes till we get these lashings on.'

'If I do that, the old man will be up straight away to see what's wrong. He's pretty worn out too, you know. He's been pushing himself as well, trying to get a trip aboard before this fish takes off. Otherwise it means a long steam north.' Ben adjusted the course on the automatic pilot.

'Well, you'll just have to go and tell him what we're up to so he doesn't turn out. I'll watch her while you go down.'

Ben stared at me for a few moments, weighing up his options. 'OK,' he said. 'Keep an eye on the water, follow a 120-fathom and I'll be back in a few minutes.' Then he dashed down the stairway to the captain's cabin directly beneath us.

A few minutes later, I heard both captain and mate on the stairs. My heart sank. The skipper had turned out anyway and he wouldn't be best pleased. Arriving on the bridge, Dowsy looked out the window and studied the conditions, grunting with annoyance when he saw the amount of water pounding the fore-deck. 'Hummph!' he snapped. 'The weather's deteriorated. You should've got the job done long before it got as bad as this.'

Was he kidding? It was like this when he went down. As he'd have known if he'd stayed on the bridge a bit longer after ringing the ship on.

'You'd better go down with 'im and sort it out, Ben. It's your job anyway, I'll give you five minutes to get ready. When I ease her in you've got ten minutes. Then I'm ringing her on again. I want to be back at the starting-point for the dawning haul.' (On most grounds, the dawning haul usually brought the best result of the day.)

Back in the drying-room, the mate started donning his waterproofs. 'Be ready to drop down smart on deck as soon as you hear the telegraph,' he warned the crew. 'We've only got ten minutes.'

Once the ship began to ease down we all moved quickly. We spread the cod-ends again and although we were still uncomfortable, with sheets of spray sweeping over us, at least the heavy water was no longer washing us away. With the mate and I working separately on the job, we soon had it finished. The telegraph rang as we regained our feet, and we just had time to heave the cod-ends out of the way and scurry off deck before the ship picked up speed.

Returning to the drying-room, we pulled off our waterproofs. What would people think of this episode? I wondered. Might they perhaps see it as the mate finishing off a job I'd failed to complete?

Over the next few days, the skipper drove us harder than ever. Keeping the trawl down on the bottom for as long as possible, he was bringing aboard biggish hauls of fish at regular intervals, and testing my reduced lung power to the full. Eventually though, the catches began to dwindle. Although we'd a reasonable trip aboard, it still wasn't enough for a ship of this size and Dowsy decided to carry on further north to the neighbouring grounds, off the island of Fruholmen. The white fish would probably have left this area as well, but we might find some coal fish, more commonly known as coley, which usually held on longer. Although very palatable, coley was considered second-class and usually made only half the price of white fish.

We hung around off Fruholmen, taking nothing more than fair-size hauls of coley. That told me all I needed to know. For Johnny Dowsam, it wasn't so much about the money as the size of the catch, whatever the kind of fish. Johnny was after the Silver Cod, the prize awarded to the boat landing the most fish in any one year. Luckily for him, the coley held on for another two or three days, and we left for home with close to a full ship, landing one day shorter than expected.

Although by no means ebullient, Dowsy did seem reasonably pleased as we made our way home. After all, we did have over 3000 ten-stone kits of fish on board. But with nearly 800 kits of coley among them, the skipper couldn't be completely satisfied and would obviously be looking to make changes. The day before we docked, I was on watch on the bridge, when Dowsy called me into the chart-room. 'Look, Rob,' he began. 'I know this has been a tough trip for you after such a long lay-off. Perhaps we were expecting a bit too much of you in a ship this size so soon after your illness. You might be better signing off and finding a smaller ship to re-establish yourself. I'll speak to Gibby and ask him to find you a smaller ship to start with. What do you say?'

I shrugged my shoulders. 'OK, Skipper. If that's what you think. I'm sorry if I've not come up to your expectations.'

'No, that's not the point,' Dowsy interrupted me. 'I know what you can do. But I can't make this ship pay without pushing you all the time and that wouldn't be fair. I'm going to give you a break.'

What makes him think the next skipper isn't going to push me just as hard? I thought.

'I'll be happy to sign you on in future,' he added, 'when you've settled into the job again.'

So ended my first trip as bosun, and a couple of days later I signed off.

We'd made a nice trip and the extra poundage due to me as bosun cheered me up no end. I was probably facing a little time at home now while I waited for a ship. As an officer I'd joined a restricted band chasing a single vacancy on each vessel, and it might take rather longer than in the past when I had been one of eight deckies. While I was laid up, I'd had the presence of mind to get my driving licence, so now I was planning to splash out on a car. How to get hold of a nice little second-hand vehicle? That was the question preoccupying me as I walked off the dock.

Approaching the swing-bridge that spanned the lock entrance from the river, I began to meet up with a number of friends and acquaintances. The bridge was suspended on studded half-moon girders, and the narrow, boarded catwalk running alongside certainly brought people together. There were always plenty of folk streaming on and off, and as it was barely wide enough for two bodies to pass friendly faces constantly confronted you.

The Lord Line building lay just beyond the bridge. No wonder then that walking towards it I spotted a very friendly face indeed. Terry was one of my closest pals. He lived near me and like me had recently been promoted bosun in a Lord Line ship. He beamed when he spotted me. We exchanged the standard fisherman's greeting, 'When did you get home?' Then, with the answer given, 'When are you going away?'

Terry had been home for a few days while his ship was surveyed and serviced. He still had a few more days to go, so we'd get a chance to spend some time together, but not today it seemed. 'I've got some business on at the moment, Bob. I'll tell you about it later. But not today, I'm going to be busy.'

'Aye aye!' I said suspiciously. 'Have you got a new girlfriend you're keeping to yourself, you sly fox?'

Terry's grin was wider than ever. 'You'll see. I'll meet you in Rayners dinner-time tomorrow. See ya.' And with that he moved further on up the dock to meet someone else – maybe a girl in one of the offices.

I carried on through the tunnel under the railway lines that traversed the landward entrance to the dock, musing on Terry's obvious delight at what seemed to be his latest conquest. I didn't have a girlfriend myself, but maybe I could steal some of his thunder if I could move smartly in the purchase of a car. Terry and I had been fairly competitive ever since our schooldays. But the problem now was this. How could I buy a car at the right price and drive it away in just twenty-four hours?

I'd seen a couple of ads in the paper with a couple of small second-hand cars for sale at a price I could afford. The cheaper of the two was advertised by a private owner for £60. The other was offered by a dealer. At £70, this car was a bit more expensive, but it boasted a reconditioned engine, or so the ad said. If I wanted to get on the road quickly, it looked like the better bet, and the engine was an added attraction.

The dealership was on Anlaby Road, just a small, simple showroom with a bare half dozen cars. All of them were reasonably priced but only one was really cheap – a little green Morris 8, four-seater, two-door, a square back with a small oblong rear window, no boot, and the spare wheel fitted to the back with a large wing-nut. The car was parked out front in a small display area on the broad sidewalk. It shone brightly and someone had cleaned it up nicely. But had I been a bit sharper I might have noticed the rust spots around the edge of the shaped mudguards and along the bottom sill.

The proprietor came bustling out when he saw my interest. 'Not a bad little looker, eh! Still nearly three months' tax on her as well. Have a look inside, she's pretty clean.'

The salesman fussed around me as I looked her over. She really was quite exciting. The bucket-seats seemed reasonably clean and, although the steering wheel had four spokes instead of the three of newer models, she did have trafficators that flicked out of the door-jamb. You worked them with a switch lever projecting from the horn housing in the centre of the wheel. You just flicked it left or right – except the right-hand one didn't work.

'It's stuck,' said the salesman, offering to fix it. 'Try starting her now. Just pull the choke out a bit and she should start first time.'

I did as he suggested but still needed two attempts to get the car going.

'That's because it's cold,' he assured me. 'But if you do have any trouble there's a starting handle in the box under the back seat. You won't need it, though. She's got a reconditioned engine under here. Come and have a look.'

Moving round to the side of the bonnet, he unhooked the folding flap and lifted it back to reveal a neat little engine, running like a sewing-machine. This was all very well, but how was I going to get the price down below £70. I told the guy I'd seen a similar vehicle advertised for sale down a nearby street with *four* months' tax paid. But he clinched the deal by dropping the price to £65 and directing me to the insurance broker next door but one – a friend who could fix me up with third party insurance for a nominal fee.

And so I became the proud owner of a car I could drive away as soon as I'd got my cover note in the morning, giving the salesman a chance to fix the trafficator, as well as a dodgy front passenger seat that had come a bit loose.

I didn't see Terry that night. No surprise there. But I did meet up with Geoff, another old shore-based friend. We went to the West Park, our local working men's club, and a favourite of Geoff's parents and other close friends. They usually had an artiste on to entertain you, then lotto, and finally a bit of dancing to records at the end of the night. And always the chance to get a girl up for a dance – if you could find one available, that is. We spent most of our time at the bar and had a lot of fun with the barmaids.

The following morning Geoff was away to work and I wasn't due to see Terry till midday, leaving plenty of time for me to collect my new car. Well new to me, anyway. Everything was in working order when I picked her up, and I'd paid cash. All I had left to do now was top her up with petrol, then it was away to show off to Terry.

Rayners was a pub on the corner of Hessle Road and West Dock Avenue, with a long bar and a smaller room at the back. Although very popular with fishermen, it wasn't a place I used regularly. Wanting to keep the car a complete surprise, I parked a little way off and went into the long bar by the corner door. No sign of Terry among the sprinkling of people inside, but his younger brother Kenny was leaning up against the bar, chatting away to a friend. Kenny raised his hand in greeting and caught my eye. 'Can I buy you a drink?' he asked as I closed with him.

'Thanks. Where's big brother then? Is he around here anywhere?'

'Who, Terry? No, I don't think so. He was out fairly early. I don't know where he went, though.'

'Is he meeting up with a new girlfriend this lunchtime?'

'I don't know. He never tells me anything.' Kenny shrugged expressively. He was a fisherman himself so they wouldn't see each other that often.

A couple of minutes later, the door from the back room opened and in strode Terry, obviously looking for me. 'Ah, there you are.' He beamed at us both. 'Come on, I want you to meet Daisy.'

'Daisy!' we echoed in unison as we followed him into the back room and straight out the side-door to the street. There he turned and faced us, gesturing towards 'Daisy'. I found myself looking past him at a fairly attractive, two-tone, blue-black, four-door Austin 7.

'That's Daisy?'

'Well, that's what I call her,' said Terry with a grin. 'She's a beaut, isn't she?'

Now it's true the car did possess some attractive features. It had a running-board for a start, the sort of thing used by the Keystone Cops in all those Hal Roach films. Its bottom half was a lovely royal blue and the top half was black, all with a beautiful gloss. I looked behind it at my green Morris with its BKY number-plate. 'Perhaps you'd like to meet Becky,' I said, with a proprietorial sweep of the hand.

Ken and Terry both swung round to observe the object of my pride. 'Is that really yours or are you just having me on?' asked Terry.

'No, it's mine all right. It's not as smart as yours, but it does have a reconditioned engine and one extra horsepower.'

'When did you get it?'

'Yesterday, actually.'

'You never said 'owt.'

'Neither did you.'

We'd both hit upon exactly the same idea, each desperate to outdo the other. Shaking with laughter, we turned away from our cars and went back inside for a drink.

CHAPTER 2

STAYING WITH THE BIG BOYS

Now both Terry and I had wheels, we decided we'd better use them to best advantage. With the weekend approaching, we could all go to Withernsea Pavilion, one of the few places that held dances on a Sunday night. It was surprising how many of the better-class, eligible girls travelled through by train from Hull. Our plan was to set off early after tea – Geoff in my car, and Kenny with Terry. And although we were admitting nothing, it would also give us a chance to test out our respective cars. Mine had the better engine, but Terry's certainly had the edge when it came to body and suspension.

Off we went down Hedon Road, very quiet on a Sunday night, and we were starting to overlap each other even before we got out of town. I put my foot down, distancing Terry. But I had to ease off on the accelerator – the amount of rattling and wobbling was just too much – and he soon began to catch up. I slammed my foot down again, this time just as we hit a bump, and Geoff jerked so violently that the front seat – the one I'd asked the car salesman to fasten down more securely – tore up from the floor beneath. Every time I accelerated, Geoff disappeared from sight, flopping on to the back seat, and every time I braked he reappeared again.

With the town, and street lighting, behind us, I put on my headlights. For a while we just managed to hang on to the lead, braving the gale coming up from below. Then my headlights failed and I really had to slow down. But if I thought my buddy was going to do likewise I was sorely mistaken. He just roared on past, leaving me battling to keep up if I wanted to use him as a guide. Eventually I had to ease up even further on the winding road, and Terry left us to struggle along alone on side-lights. We did have one very narrow escape. Taking up far more than his fair share of the road, a large lorry came round a bend and very nearly ran us off. But this was unusual round here on a Sunday night and pretty soon we came upon a village with street lights. Our chums were parked up, waiting anxiously and relieved to see us arrive in one piece. They had passed the lorry too and were worried it might have hit us.

After I'd explained what had happened, and we'd checked Geoff out for sea-sickness after all his rocking and rolling, we decided we'd gone too far to turn back. We diagnosed the problem with the headlights as a blown fuse, but the car was unfamiliar to me and the light poor, so actually replacing it was another matter. Instead we agreed that I'd follow close behind Terry and use his headlights, with Geoff staying with me to provide moral support. To fix the passenger seat, I tried wedging the spare wheel up behind it. That would stop most of the movement, and block the cold and damp flowing up from the road. Unfortunately, it would also prevent any young ladies from riding in the back seat – rather negating the object of the whole exercise. And, as Terry was later to realise, acting as my guide would also cramp his style.

We arrived at the dance-hall without further incident and found a spot in the nearly empty car-park – not too close to the grand entrance, of course, just in case we wanted to chat up a girl on a pass-out. As expected, the large ballroom was full of pretty girls, all gaily dressed and all desperate for a partner who could dance. Fortunately we had all learnt to get around the floor with a waltz or a foxtrot, so after a couple of drinks we eventually broke the ice with one or two wallflowers to get into the rhythm. I spotted a couple of girls I really fancied but they were all deliberately avoiding eye contact. Too hard to chat up, I thought, moving on swiftly. The other boys seemed to be having some luck so we didn't get too much chance to compare notes.

Eventually I spotted a fresh-faced young lady with sparkling eyes and a bright smile, her sleeveless, low-cut dress revealing a very impressive cleavage for one so young and trim. I moved in fast. 'Could I have this dance?' I asked very politely.

She looked startled, then burst into a fit of giggles, drawing her hand to her mouth in embarrassment. Seeing my surprise, she recovered herself and apologised. 'I'm sorry, I can't really do this dance. I haven't learnt it yet.'

'Well, maybe I can teach you,' my inner gentleman replied, reluctantly.

'Thanks, but no. I'd only stand on your toes. My friend Sandra knows how to do it, though. I'm sure she'd like to dance with you. Wouldn't you, Sandra?'

'Really, Tracy,' her friend admonished her. 'You don't say things like that to people.'

Now Sandra was a tall, elegant blonde – perfect make-up, styled hair and a long ball gown. The pencil-lined Cupid's bow on her beautifully shaped mouth certainly drew the eye.

'But I thought you said ...'

'Tracy, please. I'm sure this young man can make up his own mind.'

'Yes, I can,' I insisted. 'And I'd like to dance with you. That's if Tracy doesn't mind.'

'No really,' said Sandra. 'It's quite all right. I'm fine, thank you.'

'Please,' I pressed on. 'I'm sure we'd enjoy it. As long as I don't cripple you, that is.'

'Are you sure?' Sandra was beginning to waver.

'Yes, I am. Come on,' I said, grabbing her by the hand and leading her to the floor. 'Excuse us, Tracy.'

Putting my arm around her, I realised Sandra had quite a body, but it was mostly hidden by her long gown – probably what had turned me off in the first place. She looked a bit stodgy compared to the bobby-soxers, and personally I preferred the flared skirts. Why had Tracy giggled in surprise? I wondered. Was she about to suggest that her big friend was interested in me, maybe on account of my height?

Deciding Sandra and I needed to get better acquainted, I tried to snuggle in closer, but she was having none of it – pushing me off and maintaining an aloof, upright stance. Still, she seemed to want to chat. She obviously came from an affluent family and only frequented the better venues. I suppose it was the décor and ballroom atmosphere of the Pavilion that had attracted her, hence the dress. It turned out that her father owned a fish merchant's – and not any old firm either, but Johnston's, pretty much a nationwide name.

I danced more than once with Sandra. She was willing enough now, and starting to move in a little closer as she relaxed and got to know me better. However, she was still very reserved, moving and speaking cautiously, clearly reluctant to give me too much encouragement. A cold fish, I decided, making up my mind to move on. Anyway, she wasn't the sort of girl you could drive home in a rocking chair.

The night proved fruitless for us all. Just as well really. Getting home in one piece took all our concentration, with Terry – always a guy with a short attention span – braking periodically and then suddenly shooting away again. Of course, I had to return Becky to the dealer to get that floor sorted out, so I was on foot the next time I went down the dock to look for a ship.

I arrived to find a small group of men hanging around the entrance to the company yard. Something was clearly going on, but it didn't look as if any real opportunities were available. Apparently the *St Dominic*, the firm's new supership, had just returned from her first voyage. Like the *Loman*, the *Dominic* was a very large ship, but she was powered by diesel/electric, a novelty for trawlers at this time. In fact, there were only one or two other vessels like it in the port. No wonder then that no crew changes were expected. Nevertheless I resolved to go straight to the runner's office to see what Jack Gibson had to say.

Although Gibby greeted me cheerfully enough, things weren't looking promising. 'I'm not really expecting anyone to change bosun in the near future,' he told me. 'The only possibility is the *Dominic* – her bosun's injured. Still, even if the doc signs him off, the skipper would choose his replacement.'

'Fair enough, Jack. I'll come down again, say middle of next week, and see if anything's come up. Where's the *Dominic* now? I'd like to take a look at her.'

"She's outside, just a bit further up the dock.' Jack waved me on my way.

I thanked the runner, left the yard and crossed the cobbled road to the quayside, as usual littered with piles of spare gear stacked opposite each firm's office. Not too many ships moored on the south side today, I thought, as I looked up the dock. Only a single bank of vessels with the odd space – most unusual. Two-thirds of the way along, under No.3 Ice Chute, one vessel stood out from the rest. As yet unladen, still taking on stores and ice, and with the fuel barge alongside, her great sweeping bows rose up above her neighbours. But what really grabbed the attention were her extra beam and the extraordinarily large funnel whose company colours told me she was the *St Dominic*.

Moving closer, I was better able to appreciate her graceful lines, built-in accoutrements and spacious decks. Like the *Loman*, she had two picture windows on the bridge front. She certainly was a cut above the rest. Suddenly a figure appeared, climbed over the rail amidships and descended a small ladder to the quayside. It was the captain, Rowan Berkeley, the firm's top skipper. Rowan cut an immaculate figure in his pin-striped suit, somewhat out of place among the grime and clutter of an industrial dock-side. Slim and square-shouldered, Rowan was now in his mid- to late-fifties. Slightly less than six-feet tall, he had close-cropped, crinkly hair, greying at the sides, and clean-cut, weather-beaten features. Dusting his hands fussily, he turned and spotted me.

'Hello, young Rob!' he called. 'What are you doing just now?' I knew Rowan well and had been in his company on numerous occasions.

'Hi, Rowan. I'm out of a ship at the moment.' I turned and walked with him as we picked our way off the quay around two massive 700-fathom coils of three-inch wire warp, about to be put aboard another ship as towing lines for the trawl.

'You've got your bosun's ticket now, I understand.'

'I've got my mate's ticket actually but I'm sailing as bosun to get more experience.'

'Good,' said the skipper. 'How would you like to sign on with me then? Just for the one trip mind. Ted Newton, my regular bosun, has damaged his ankle and he needs a trip off to get it right.'

'Why cheers, Skip. That'd be great. I'd love the chance to sail on this beautiful ship.'

'OK then. Come on, we'll go and tell Jack Gibby. But don't call me Skip.'

Gibby was flabbergasted when Rowan led me into his office and told him to sign me on. I couldn't help thinking about Johnny Dowsam. So the *Loman* was too big for me, eh! At six-feet three, my height was one of the reasons I was offered the chance to sail in these large, modern ships. And the *St Dominic* wasn't just big, she was superb in every respect: the accommodation, the bridge lay-out with its special telegraphs, the electric winch, maybe too powerful, and most of all the engine room.

Entering this space, I found it hard to appreciate that I was aboard a side-trawler. Far from the one engine I was expecting, there were three. Three Mirrlees diesel engines side by side, all designed to generate the energy needed to drive the big electric motor. Looking around at the two very large switchboards, plus all the other extra equipment required to sustain this massive machine-shop, I wondered how we could ever catch enough fish to pay for it.

The crew all looked to be up to scratch. As you'd expect in a new ship, most were top men. Mate John Warren had been with Rowan for quite some time and was anticipating a skipper's job of his own pretty soon. No doubt the gaffers wanted him to help get the new ship established before he moved on. Like the skipper, he was a smart, well-spoken individual. Luckily for me he was well-organised too, if not particularly forceful.

At sea Rowan Berkeley's demeanour came as little surprise. During the morning watch, some time after breakfast, he would call the bridge on the intercom alongside his bunk and order a coffee. Then five minutes later he would appear, clad in corduroy trousers, sponge-soled brogues and a smart shirt, tying his neckerchief in a bow at the side of his neck. He usually ignored the wheelman or look-out, but he would acknowledge the officer with a curt good morning.

Even though the *Dominic* had a smart new bridge with highly polished panelling and bright new chrome fittings, Rowan appeared to handle everything with his finger-tips. It looked as if he didn't want to dirty or damage his hands. Lord knows how he had behaved when he was mate. But our old man was no softy by any means. As we were soon to find out, he was hard, ruthless and resourceful in his quest for a successful trip.

Myself apart, there were two or three other additions to the crew, among them a rather unusual galley boy. Darren was a big, heavy-shouldered six-footer, clearly from an affluent family. He boarded wearing a camel-hair raglan coat, carrying a quality suitcase instead of a kit-bag, and accompanied by a very attractive, university-type girl. He was probably at university himself, although his long, blond, sleeked-back hair made him look smarter than the average student. But appearances can be deceptive. Looking smart doesn't necessarily mean that you are smart, or hard-working for that matter.

Chances are that Darren had heard about the money to be earned fishing, but the operative word here is earned. As galley boy, he would be expected to help the cook in every way – peeling potatoes, washing pots, setting tables, cleaning mess decks and store-rooms, and generally doing all the fetching and carrying. Always providing, of course, he could conquer any sea-sickness. And for this he would receive a basic wage each week, more than the average apprentice ashore, but certainly no compensation for the hours expected of him. He would get no share in the trip and, unless the crew agreed to it, nothing of the liver money from the cod-liver oil we landed. All he could expect, if he looked after the crew and maybe cleaned their accommodation once in a while, would be back-handers or tips.

Sea-sickness proved no problem for Darren. However, it soon became clear that he wasn't interested in doing anyone a favour, indeed in doing any work at all. We saw very little of him in the officers' mess amidships. He set the tables, after a fashion, in time for meals, but he never cleared them properly afterwards – copping a couple of warnings from me as a result. But over in the crew's mess things were much worse. He moved slowly and reluctantly, and the lads were always on at him because cutlery and other items were missing from the table. Poor old cook did his best to keep on top of him, but for much of the time the galley boy was nowhere to be found. I was chasing out the daymen after breakfast one morning when I caught him stretched out at the table on one of the long seats.

'What on earth do you think you're up to?' I asked him.

'Getting my breakfast, of course,' he replied. And to prove his point, Darren propped himself up on one elbow and picked up a handy knife which he used to stab a slice of bread, then neatly flick the lid off a jar of marmalade and ladle some onto his breakfast. He then stuffed the whole lot into his mouth before finally sinking back down again. Minimum effort, maximum effect. He was turning laziness into an art form.

As the voyage continued things went from bad to worse. The big galley hand showed little respect for anyone and only narrowly avoided a couple of thumpings. Then one day he really overstepped the mark. Fed up with all the jeers and the harassment, Darren cleared off to his bunk in the middle of the day, shut himself away, and lay there playing with himself, regardless of anything the cook could say or do. It was difficult to rive him out because he was in a lower bunk, although one or two did try. Even the mate went in to warn him. But in the meantime the little cook had gone off to find the old man. Pretty soon Rowan appeared from the bridge and came marching down the alley-way towards the double berth. In went the skipper and out came the mate. Then Rowan strode out of the cabin and crossed the alley-way to the galley, returning with a large bucket of cold water.

An almighty splash, then exit the captain back down the alley-way. Another slight pause, then exit one galley boy, very bedraggled and dragging a soaking mattress behind him. What Rowan said to him, nobody knows. But if he hadn't mended his ways, I rather fancy the young crewman would have gone pretty hungry thereafter.

Rowan Berkeley, as you would expect, was a fine fisherman. He was still pursuing the quality fish, even though it was almost midsummer, when the fishing traditionally becomes slack, and he moved on regularly, looking for bigger and better hauls. He often called me to the bridge after the fish was down below and I picked up a lot from the clever skipper. But I also learned something else on the *St Dominic* which later became very important to me.

Even though we sometimes fished thousands of miles from home, we hadn't yet started freezing the catch. Instead we packed it in ice to land as fresh fish, and the White Fish Authority had chosen the *Dominic* to carry out some trials to discover the best method of preserving fish at sea. Each shelved section of the fish-room had been fitted out with thermometer probes, wired back to monitoring equipment temporarily placed in a spare walk-in cupboard close to my berth amidships. Two scientists had joined us on this particular trip, placing probes into selected fish as the catch was packed away, and recording the temperature of the cargo in every part of the fish-hold.

With the two scientists working close to my accommodation, I was in an ideal position to quiz them. What was the warmest part of the fish-room at different points in the trip? What was the best way to preserve fish?

What you need to do, these two boffins told me, is encase each fish individually in ice and never allow it to touch its neighbours – information which later stood me in good stead, when as mate I found myself in charge of preserving the fish.

Of course, all this was a lot to ask, so quickly did the haul pour down the hatch, and with only three men down below to crack ice, lay shelves and direct different fish into separate pounds. I thought I had the answer – up to a point anyway – but I would need the chance to prove it.

John, the mate, took a different attitude. To him, these guys were nothing but a nuisance, and he never took the chance to learn from them. I could understand his feelings, though. While the mate and his fish-room man were striving to keep pace with the downpour, these two were putting them under extra strain, constantly interrupting their work by jumping in the fish-pounds to insert the probes.

Meanwhile our skipper continued to pursue the top-quality fish so scarce at this time of the year. Apparently ships were steaming all over the Barents Sea in search of a reasonable catch so any captain who found one would be keeping it to himself. As the firm's top skipper, Rowan had a reputation to maintain. But this does not mean that he always behaved impeccably and set an example to his peers. Rowan, like any skipper, was prepared to take chances when things were getting desperate.

Our sparks had picked up a report that two ships were catching some decent hauls by towing tight along the limit-line off Hjelmsøy, an island close to the North Cape, and Rowan decided to look it over for himself. Approaching the Cape, we passed odd ships dotted all along the limit-line, in water varying in depth from 120 to 140 fathoms. Eventually we identified the two ships in question, stopped, shot our gear and towed up to them. They turned out to be Hull vessels, so Rowan was soon able to establish contact. Although their echo-sounders were showing good signs, the fish were apparently going down in numbers only for the dawning haul, which was realising sixty to seventy baskets. Still, it was all excellent quality fish. So we towed along with our two Hull colleagues, at 125 to 130 fathoms, sometimes scraping along the limit-line as measured by radar.

A fisheries protection gunboat was steaming up and down trying to cover as much of the area as possible. However, with ships scattered right along the line, he was coming and going at regular intervals. We took one or two poor hauls, then shot away again after tea. This was traditionally the mate's watch below so it was no surprise when Rowan called me to the bridge. But I was astonished when I found out what he had in mind.

With darkness falling, the skipper wanted me to observe the gunboat through the binoculars as it steamed easily away down the line. 'Take a good look at his deck and accommodation lights, Bob. Study them so you can recognise them in the dark if he comes back in a hurry. Then I want you to pick him up on the radar and plot him constantly 'cos I'm going to be busy for the next hour or so. You said you got top marks at radar school, didn't you?'

It was true, I had done well there. Although it isn't easy to plot vessels accurately, I found it was something that came naturally to me.

I jammed my face into the radar visor, working with cursor and rangefinder to keep the target in view, while Rowan concentrated on steering the ship and watching the compass and echo-sounder. Every now and then he would push me out of the way to check on our distance from land. 'Let me know if he starts heading back this way,' he warned me, 'or if you lose him.'

I knew now what Rowan was planning. He was going to make a sweep inside the limit-line to check out the prospects in the shoaler water. The fading light would make it difficult for anyone else to tell what he was up to. And that included the crew – myself excepted, of course.

For the next hour or so I kept close watch on one particular echo, constantly glancing around the darkening horizon to see what our companions were doing. I soon had my answer: they were all staying on the right side of the law. On screen, Hjelmsøy drew ever closer. And, as the bottom shoaled on the echograph paper, the clumps of fish were clearly becoming more dense. The skipper spent an hour allowing the ship to skirt around the edge of the shoaling bank in a depth of ninety-five to a hundred fathoms. Then I told him I was losing the echo from the edge of the screen about fourteen miles off.

'OK, Bob. It'll take him at least forty-five minutes to get back to us. We'll double back for half an hour, then head over the line again and see what we've got. Watch that bearing a bit longer, then you can go for a drink before we haul.' The skipper turned the ship round, deliberately directing it towards the land and shoaling the water a little, his excitement growing as he watched the fish. Eventually, he turned away and headed back to the limit-line, dismissing me from the bridge in search of my promised drink.

Before long the telegraph rang to warn us all it was hauling time and the gear came to the surface with an almighty whoosh. The cod-ends shot out, jam-packed with fish, then laid out on the water with the bellies also full.

That'll mean another jaunt inside the line for sure, I thought.

The haul produced four big bags, all good fish, and all of fifty to sixty baskets each, so well over two hundred baskets in all – nearly a day's work in itself. Once we'd paid the gear away again, Rowan called me back to the bridge. The boys weren't happy – after all they'd been a man short gutting our first big haul – but I couldn't tell them what was going on.

After manoeuvring to get the four bags aboard and the gear shot away, we could no longer be sure the gunboat was still off the screen, so Rowan spent the first twenty minutes edging his way over the limit while we checked on what everyone else was doing. Unfortunately for us, they were all still skirting the line, identifying it pretty clearly on the screen – and equally any encroachment we might make.

But Rowan was in the mood to take a chance. Heedless of any danger, he plunged straight in towards the land. Meanwhile I kept constant vigil on the south-western quarter of the radar screen, where I had last sighted the navy ship. This time the skipper swept further in, shoaling as far as the eighty-fathom mark where the fish appeared even more plentiful, and making me more nervous still. Should the gunboat return, we were now even further away from the limit-line and safety.

With so much fish showing, Rowan decided to cut down on our towing time and we proceeded without mishap. By now midnight had come and gone, so the mate had come to the bridge to relieve the skipper. This was normal practice, but this situation was far from normal. Having studied the radar for the last hour and a half, I had developed a feel for things as targets hauled and steamed and shifted position. Conveying all this to the mate would be both tedious and time-consuming, especially as we were now heading back towards the line. The skipper told John what was happening and asked him instead to go down and supervise the last of the fish.

We were soon across the line again, and preparing to haul, when the skipper came up with another surprise. 'Hold on here while we bring the gear aboard, Bob. I can't manoeuvre the ship and keep an eye on the screen while we're hauling, particularly when we're swinging round. If you'll keep an eye on things, and if you're satisfied no unusual targets are approaching, I'll shoot straight in towards land once we've got the fish aboard.'

I was a little embarrassed to find myself on the bridge like this while the mate worked the deck, and not a little nervous at the amount of responsibility this conferred upon me. If caught inside the limit-line with our fishing gear unstowed, the gunboat would arrest us and take us in. The result – a fine for the skipper and the ship, and probably the confiscation of our gear. Hardly a great example to set for the younger skippers. But if Rowan got away with it and caught a trip when others didn't, it would only confirm his position as top dog.

Despite the reduced towing time, our last haul realised five bags of fish, and it needed some manoeuvring to bring it all in. I continued to watch the screen closely, trying to monitor any extra targets that approached – difficult with the ship swinging about. But at last the fish was all aboard.

'Anything suspicious?' asked Rowan. 'If not, I'm shooting straight in to save time while it's still dark.'

Identifying suspicious targets on a radar screen is easier said than done. Unless they're very large, nearly all ships appear as a dot. I could only identify the gunboat by its speed and method of approach. If a target approached at speed inside the line of ships, and therefore inside the limit-line, it must be the gunboat. Of course, the gunboat would also be able to spot us on the screen. But he would have to get close enough to identify us, hence Rowan operating under cover of darkness.

'No obvious danger,' I told the skipper timorously. 'A couple of new targets have appeared recently, but they're coming from a safe direction.'

'Good!' And Rowan rang the telegraph to proceed.

Once we'd circled and lowered the gear, Rowan rang the ship on full speed and shot straight in towards Hjelmsøy, streaming the gear behind. I watched the screen even more avidly but I couldn't resist an occasional glance towards the depth recorder, which showed the bottom rapidly shoaling. With the towing warps safely secured in the towing block, Rowan lined the ship up at the appropriate depth and continued to follow it for the next hour and a half. He had found exactly what he was looking for – the darkness just before dawn, the time when the fish go down to feed.

At this time of year, dawn in these northern latitudes comes at around three o'clock, so this would be our last tow of the night. Over the next hour or so things became a bit tense as the skipper devoted all his attention to keeping the *Dominic* in the right water, offering me no help whatsoever when the targets began to scatter as if becoming restless. Then another target appeared just beyond them, and from the critical south-western edge of the screen. Although apparently heading in our direction, it did not appear to be inside the line. Was it just another trawler steaming to the grounds? Plotting its speed over the next few minutes might give me the answer, but I had to report the sighting to the skipper straight away.

For the first time Rowan came over to the screen. In the short term, the target presented no problem, but he acknowledged my concern. 'See if you can work out its speed, Bob. I just want a few more minutes to get to the edge of the bank. Then I'll head for the line before he gets too close. It could be the gunboat trying to fool us by keeping among the other ships.'

I tried to concentrate. Measuring distance and bearing, I reckoned the target was approaching pretty quickly, but maybe no faster than some of the modern trawlers. Five full minutes of observation would be needed before I could work out its hourly speed. Just head straight for the limit-line now, I pleaded silently with the skipper. But Rowan must have worked out how much time he had to spare if the target did turn out to be a gunboat.

With the five minutes nearly up, we suddenly heard a terrible screeching sound from the winch brakes, and the towing warps began to pull out. Oh no, we'd come fast on the bottom! We were going nowhere until we could clear the trawl from the fastener on the sea-bed. With our ship stopped dead in the water, I tried to reassess the movements of the new target. But we didn't stay still for long. On the skipper's instructions, the warps were knocked out of the block and the winch began hoving the ship back towards the fastener. Should I stay where I was or go down on deck? I was unsure, but I decided to stick with my last order until told otherwise.

We were now right over the top of the gear, see-sawing back and forth as the fastener clung on. Time was passing and we were still stuck well over the line. 'How far away is that ship now?' Rowan blurted out, staring down through the bridge window at the straining warps, his hand on the telegraph.

I measured the distance and passed on the information he required. 'The target isn't coming straight towards us. It looks as if he's heading towards the point where we'll cross the line. I'm not sure he's aware we're in difficulty.'

Just then the gear let go of the bottom and at last we could start to heave it to the surface. 'Better get down there and give 'em a hand,' the skipper ordered. 'I'll watch the radar now we're stopped.'

I left the bridge, donned my waterproofs and dropped down on deck to work the after end, while the mate took charge forr'ard. With a bit of luck we could scramble the gear aboard quickly and get steaming full speed for the line. Then the trawl shot to the surface and spread out. It was bulging with fish. God, there were more than ever! We'd barely towed for an hour and a quarter and it looked like we'd taken six bags. We'd need all of twenty minutes to get it aboard, time we just didn't have.

With the skipper, mate and I all screaming like banshees, the men were running frantically around the deck. The fish piled aboard, covering the fore-deck, and with each new bag I was scanning the darkened horizon in search of approaching lights. Then the first light of dawn began to appear slowly in the east: in another half hour our cover would be gone. It seemed an eternity before we could finally ring the ship on.

'Lift the trawl doors in board,' the skipper shouted down to the mate and me. 'Try to secure as much of the gear as possible. We need to look legal. And find some tarpaulin or hatch covers to cover the fish.'

What, with this lot! Was he kidding? This ship had steel hatches so we'd only have a couple of tarpaulins aboard. Perhaps we could use spare net instead? We worked on, the *Dominic* speeding for the line, while I glanced anxiously over the port bow where the target would most likely appear. Outlined against the lightening sky, the other trawlers were just beginning to emerge in silhouette. Then I saw another vessel approaching at speed. It definitely wasn't a trawler, and the position of the other ships suggested that we weren't yet over the line.

I stopped what I was doing and perched on top of the mound of fish in an effort to make it out. Of course, the rest of the crew were ignorant of our situation, so they worked on oblivious to our peril as I squinted at the oncoming vessel with its short fore-deck. What disgrace for Rowan if he was arrested for poaching. And what trauma for us all if they also confiscated the fish and the gear.

Then came a voice behind me. 'It's a tug.' I turned around to find Rowan grinning over his binoculars at me from the bridge window. 'It's an ocean-going tug,' he repeated. 'It must be dashing to its next job. It certainly won't be interested in finding out who we are. But I think we'll give this place a rest and look somewhere else.' I couldn't have agreed more.

The sparks had heard reports of a decent bag to be had in and around some foul ground on Cape Bank. Rowan knew this ground better than most, and it was only five hours distant, but it would take us all that time to clear this mound of fish. 'Click, click' I heard repeatedly from the crew as we dug into the side of the writhing mass covering the deck. Experience told me what was going on. Deckies used the expression to suggest the skipper was taking a photo of one of their number. Or that's how they put it if they spotted a member of the gutting squad constantly looking up at the bridge and posing on the job.

Their target was Jocky McCann. Jock fancied himself a speedster when it came to gutting, and he was working away, facing aft and exaggerating every move he made. Every skipper wanted men like him in their team because clearing the fish was a constant headache when the big catches came aboard. Small and wiry, Jock had sailed with Rowan for quite a while now. Although he had his bosun's ticket, he had seldom obtained a start – perhaps because he lacked vision and imagination, and he was clearly unable to organise men. Nevertheless, he must have been expecting to get his opportunity on this trip. And, like many who knew about my illness, he would no doubt have been wondering if I was fit enough to do the job. Fingers crossed, I hadn't been found wanting up to now.

Once again Rowan Berkeley came up trumps. His knowledge of the foul ground on the Cape Bank, littered with fastenings and marine-life puddings, was unsurpassed. These puddings covered the bottom in great numbers and would chafe out both fish and net if caught in any quantity. You had to know their position to make sure you avoided them and stayed with the fish, something Rowan did with aplomb. Added to our great start, he was once again in a position to set off for home with more fish aboard than anyone else. Standing aft on the after deck of the *Dominic*, in full view of those on the dock-side, I was full of pride when we arrived home. With a trip full of quality fish about to bring top prices we could be sure we'd soon be in the money.

I was lucky enough to do two trips in the *Dominic* before Bosun Newton returned. Rowan was happy with my work and it was all good experience for me.

CHAPTER 3

GOOD, BAD OR RIDICULOUS – IT'S ALL EXPERIENCE

In the money, but out of a ship again. Still, I'd have some time at home to use my car – or so I thought. I just couldn't get her started. I'd been leaving her on some spare grass opposite the house and the damp must have got in. I had to remove the spark plugs, warm them up to dry them, and then use the starting handle with the choke right out. Once I'd got her going, she gave me no more trouble – for the time being at least.

Terry was home – great – and I was glad I could drive round and see him. He too was looking forward to using his car, so we decided on a run out that evening to a pub or a dance. We might even manage to pick up some girls! Friday night was concert night at the Ferry Boat Inn – perfect for us. The Ferry Boat usually held a barn dance on its wooden dance floor, and that meant plenty of girls. Situated on the bank of the Humber, down a little creek known as Hessle Haven, the old inn was rather out of the way. It was a perfect setting, far enough from any residential areas to play country and western music at a good volume – something which soon became evident as we drew up on some spare grass alongside the creek to the strains of Rosemary Clooney belting out 'This Old House'. The skiffle group that usually played was probably taking a break.

A lively scene greeted us as we stepped into the long barn-like room. A long bar ran along the back wall; to our right, tables were laid out to cover over a good half of the space available; and to our left was a slightly raised stage with musical instruments set out upon it, and a large, rough-planked area for dancing. A number of couples occupied the floor, mostly girls jiving to records, and it was no surprise to see several shipmates past and present sprinkled among the tables. The Ferry Boat was one of several large pubs that held concert nights on different days of the week, a magnet for fishermen during their short spells at home.

Over by one of the curtained windows Terry's brother and cousin had their hands in the air, trying to attract our attention. They were sitting at a table for six, along with their respective girlfriends and two other girls, both very attractive, and we started edging around the dance floor towards them. A girl jiving nearby turned her head and smiled at me. 'Hi, Bob. Long time, no see.' I muttered a reply, still unable to place her. Then it came back to me, her name was Irene. We'd met up two or three years ago, before my illness, and enjoyed a congenial association in someone's house. She was hot stuff, and I wondered if she was free.

Terry grabbed a couple of chairs for us and we pulled up alongside the two pretty girls, Debbie and Jean. I was sitting next to Debbie, a petite blonde with wavy hair cropped below the ear and flicked out at the bottom. She had flawless skin, glossy lips and even white teeth, and looked very open with her sparkling blue eyes. She giggled at everything, especially the suggestive jokes, and was obviously a fun-loving girl. She didn't seem to have had much experience of men, though. Thoughts of Irene were fading fast.

Debbie had been drinking cider, but her friend Jean – clearly much more assured – had just persuaded her to try a vodka and orange, which she was now sipping warily. We chatted and joked happily together until we'd finished the next round of drinks. Then the band returned and the barn dance continued. We all decided to get up and give it a try. None of us lads knew what we were doing, but we tried to follow the caller and whirled our partners round at devilish speed, with much merriment and laughter. As the night went on, Debbie became much happier to grab hold of her partner as instructed, and I wasn't so dozy with my do-si-dos. We were both steaming by the time the caller began to sing 'The Last Waltz with You' and we clung together recovering our breath, each very much aware of the other's body.

The dancing finished as usual at five to ten – the Ferry Boat was one of those pubs on the outskirts of town whose position allowed it the extra half hour's drinking time. But Debbie and I had only one thing in mind as we walked from the dance floor, our arms around each other, and that was to cool off outside. The night was balmy, a full moon shining out of an almost clear sky as we headed across the road towards the creek. We admired the silvery edges of the odd fluffy cloud drifting by, but I'd parked my car behind a clump of trees which shielded the river from view.

'If you want to jump in my car, we could drive clear of the trees and see the moon in the water,' I suggested.

'Car?' said Debbie. 'You have a car?' She looked up at me with a glint in her eye, gaping in disbelief. No surprise there; very few people of our age had their own car in 1958.

'Yeah, sure. Come on, I'll show you. We'll go for a little ride.' We walked the few yards back to my little Morris. Debbie was thrilled with the car, as well as the prospect of maybe having a boyfriend with wheels for future dates. 'Come on, get in,' I prompted her.

Debbie needed no more encouragement. She was in a romantic haze, the result no doubt of the unaccustomed liquor she'd been consuming. I knew exactly where we could go, close to the river's edge and far from prying eyes. Less than half a mile up the road was a chalk quarry, now virtually abandoned, known locally as Little Switzerland. A small part of the quarry was still operational, but it was away on the far side and completely screened by scrub.

I reversed out and accelerated away. As I changed into top gear, I glanced in my mirror and fancied I saw another couple crossing the road behind us. They were heading for the same clump of trees we had just left, but my view was obscured by a passing cloud.

I tucked the car behind a bush. Then Debbie and I walked hand in hand down to the river and settled in some long grass. Snuggling up close, I put my arm around her waist and pulled her into the hollow of my shoulder. 'Just look at that,' I whispered, as we gazed across the broad sweep of the Humber to the opposite bank, over a mile away. A full moon shone brightly on the indigo waters, while a fractured silver strip led directly towards us, reflecting across the full width of the river. Meanwhile the Humber flowed silently by, ripples showing here and there as glittering reflections of flashing moonlight.

Debbie sighed, allowing her forehead to lean against my chin, and my arm tightened around her waist. Her blouse, a simple white affair with puffed sleeves, rode up from her skirt as I clutched her close, and I could feel the satin smoothness of her skin beneath. I turned my head towards her, nudging her forehead back with my chin until she was looking straight up at me. The moon was reflected in her eyes, making them glisten and soften in welcome, and I leaned forward to kiss those generous lips. My other hand slid up to her tummy, massaging it gently, before carrying on towards her firm, pert breasts. Debbie's hand grasped the back of my neck as we supped and nuzzled, pulling me closer and seemingly offering her bosom for exploration.

Woof, woof! A dog was barking close by, and it sounded like a big one. Debbie stiffened immediately. A shout followed. 'Come here.' Someone, probably the security guard, was trying to retrieve the hound. Ruff, ruff! Bow wow! Now the dog was crashing through the undergrowth, no doubt after a rabbit. But Debbie wasn't hanging about, she was already up and off. And unfamiliar with the area she was running in the wrong direction! I jumped up to give chase, grabbed her by the wrist and dragged her back towards the car. But passing at speed in front of a big bush, another couple appeared directly in front of us and we collided heavily.

'Ouf! Fucking hell, Terry! What are you doing here?'

'Same as you, you mucky bugger. We saw you leave.'

It's unlikely our partners heard the exchange – the dog was making too much of a racket. Certainly nothing more was said as we raced on towards our respective cars. But then Debbie yelped. She'd stubbed her toe on a rock and only my grip saved her from a fall. It must have hurt terribly in those open-toed shoes. Heroically, she stumbled on to the car and sanctuary, and we were able to zoom off into the night.

Debbie did what she could to examine the damage in the confines of the front seat, the blood on her hand showing that she had a nasty cut. I reached into my pocket as I drove away and passed her a clean handkerchief to wrap up her toe and stem the bleeding. It was obvious to us both that if we were entertaining any other romantic notions for the rest of the night they were out. I had to get Debs home for some attention.

Fortunately, she lived only fifteen minutes away, down Division Road, one of the better streets in the west end of town. I escorted my date from the car, propping her up as she hopped to her front door. Suddenly she grabbed hold of my ears and gave me a big, smoochy kiss. 'Thanks for helping me,' she said. 'And for being such a gentleman.'

You can thank the dog for that, I thought.

'I go to the Newington every Thursday. Perhaps we can meet up again there.' (The Newington was the local dance hall.) I figured since she lived so close to the fish dock we were bound to meet up again anyway.

I was feeling pretty satisfied with my progress as bosun. I'd already sailed in two top ships with two top skippers, learnt a lot and put a fair bit of money in the bank. But now I was expecting to be out of a ship for a while. Bosun's berths were few and far between, and there were plenty of men looking to sign on, especially with summer almost upon us. I decided to keep my money even tighter, cut down on the pubs and the dance halls, and concentrate on studying from my *Fisherman's Handy Billy* and navigation books until my friends came home or a cheap night out offered itself.

Just such an opportunity soon presented itself. I still went to St Andrew's Dock most mornings to keep myself in Gibby's mind when the chances came along, and going down by car on my next visit took me off my normal route in search of a parking space. The other entrance to the dock, via what was known as the T bridge, took me past yards I didn't often visit, and I bumped into another chum, Eddie Woolford. Eddie was the same age as me and we had both sat for our bosun's ticket at the same time. Furthermore, our fathers were both skippers, though mine had retired and was now ship's husband with our firm.

Eddie stepped towards me as I went past. 'Now then, Bob,' he said with a grin. 'What ship are you in?'

'Hi, Eddie! Nothing for now. I've just come out of the *St Dominic*.'

Eddie was suitably impressed. 'Been in the big ones, eh? Well, if you're home for a while same as me, are you going to the Fish Merchants' Ball next week?

'Don't think so. I'm trying to save up a bit until I can get a regular ship.'

'That's OK. Your old man is bound to be invited. Why don't you ask him if you can go along? He's hardly likely to ask you to pay for the extra ticket. Then all it'll cost you is the price of a round and you'll get a free meal and some wine. There'll be some pretty girls there, Bob. They'll be crying out for a dancing partner.'

'Mmm, it's a thought. Sounds quite attractive.'

'You bet it does.' Eddie was really enthusiastic. 'For a start Ash is at home at the moment so Janine will be there.'

'Ash' was the nickname of one of Hull's top skippers. Though no oil painting himself, I knew that his daughter Janine was the apple of many a young man's eye, and decided to follow up on Eddie's idea.

The Fish Merchants' Dinner and Dance was held at the Skyline Ballroom at the top of the new Co-operative Building in the centre of town, and I was happy to go along with my parents and check it out. We'd been seated at a round table for ten, and to my delight they'd put us together with Skipper Ashburn and his wife and daughter, so I was sharing a table with the very girl Eddie had mentioned. Also with us was that well-known fish merchant Andrew Johnston, accompanied by his wife – and his daughter Sandra.

The elegant Sandra was my immediate neighbour and looked bound to keep me in conversation all night. She looked lovely, and we were, of course, already acquainted, after dancing together at the Withernsea Pavilion, but I'd already decided she was a little too reserved for my liking. I wanted to concentrate my attentions instead on the pretty, dark-haired, vivacious Janine opposite. How on earth could I make her realise that Sandra and I were not a couple?

As time wore on I was becoming more and more frustrated as a succession of young men came across and asked Janine to dance. She kept smiling at me, suggesting that I'd be successful too, if only I would ask. But our parents seemingly expected me to partner Sandra whenever the music struck up. So too did Sandra, asking me for a dance each time I was about to make my move. So cool on our first meeting, Sandra was surprisingly animated that night, offering me a limp hand each time she rose from her seat. Still, she was an eye-catcher, with her expensive, off-the-shoulder dress exposing milky, blemish-free flesh and tantalising indications of firm, well-shaped breasts.

At last Sandra went to the cloakroom and I finally managed to get a dance with Janine. She was a delight. Smaller than Sandra, her curves were even more accentuated, and she was so lively with her sparkling eyes and ready laugh. Sandra returned to find Janine and I still dancing and didn't look best pleased. Nothing was said, but her body certainly made much greater contact with mine in the dances that followed.

Needless to say, both girls left with their parents so I had no opportunity to escort either of them home, and I took pains to point this out to little Eddie when I encountered him, also escort-less, as we were leaving. 'OK, so things didn't work out this time,' he said. 'Don't worry, though. There's a dance at the university next week. It's really just for students and you know how radgy they are. But I've got an invite and I can take you along if you like.'

'That might be a bit of an eye-opener,' I replied. 'Sure, count me in.'

'Great! I'll be in touch with the details,' said Eddie, and he moved off into the night.

I spent a very quiet weekend, choosing to save money by studying in my room and playing my modern, eight-stack, auto play, portable record player, and looking forward to the university dance. On Monday seven ships were landing – two of them ours – so I thought I'd better go down the dock just in case. One of the two was the *St Amant*, a trawler of the old single-bridge type. It had a foc's'le forr'ard but was otherwise a nice ship, comfortable and fast. The bosun slept aft anyway, in a bunk in the officers' mess cabin. The other ship was the *St Leger*, a double-bridger built a few years back and commanded by Dusty Rhodes, one of the older skippers. Dusty had been with the *Leger* since she was built, always with the same crew.

The two crews were waiting at the entrance when I arrived at the yard and I started chatting with some guys I'd sailed with or knew from elsewhere. I intended to nip into Gibby's office when he was less busy and ask what the chances were. I wasn't expecting anything – even in the *Amant* – but it was always sensible to keep in the runner's line of sight. Before I could make a move, out came Gibby. He called me into his office, his face devoid of expression. 'There's a bosun's slot going in the *St Leger*. Are you interested?' Meanwhile in the background his assistant Benny was grinning away.

'Am I interested?' I gasped. 'Is the Pope Catholic? What do you think?'

'Well, grab a pen then,' said Jack, with a smirk. 'She sails day after tomorrow. Four a.m.'

I left the office chuffed but rather apprehensive: Dusty Rhodes seldom made any crew changes. I had never sailed with him before but they reckoned he was easy-going enough. I never thought to ask why the other bosun had chucked it. I knew Dusty's son sailed as his third hand so it looked like I'd be very much the outsider.

Then I had another thought. I wouldn't be around for the students' dance.

What a shame. Better warn Eddie. I set off quickly down the dock. Perhaps Eddie would be outside his firm's office. Suddenly I had so much to do. That was the trouble with this job. You never knew when you were going to be whisked away. Eddie, however, was nowhere to be seen. 'He's already been and gone,' said a couple of the lads waiting outside. All I could do then was leave a message to say I'd signed on, then I hurried away.

It bothered me a bit that I couldn't let Eddie know. I pictured him trying and failing to contact me, then having to attend the party on his own. But I couldn't waste any more time searching for him; I'd too much to do myself. Two days later I boarded the *St Leger* in the early hours of the morning. As bosun, I was able to proceed directly to the officers' accommodation, climbing the stairwell amidships from the deck to the first veranda. My cabin was right in the middle of the ship, opposite the mate and directly beneath the captain, with the officers' small mess-room just foreside of us. Entering the accommodation from that first veranda, I went right past the skipper's berth, but there was no sign of him. He probably hadn't arrived yet.

Approaching this area from aft took you over the top of the engine room via a catwalk which I traversed after sorting out my gear. Any fears I had about my reception by the crew were soon confirmed when I passed by their mess on my way aft. Sticking my head in to say good morning, I received nothing but a fish-eyed stare in response. Proceeding aft, I stepped out on the after deck on the starboard side, where we were moored to the quay, and lit a cig. I was watching dawn approaching, and idly studying the fastenings of the stern and spring ropes, when a taxi pulled up alongside forr'ard and I got my first chance to study the skipper at close quarters.

Dusty Rhodes was a thick set, podgy man in his fifties, slightly under six feet tall. His heavy shoulders probably stemmed from his days as a mate. With his baggy suit, coat unbuttoned, and an open-necked shirt beneath a home-knitted Fair Isle pullover, he cut a rather unkempt figure. The morning breeze ruffled his unbrushed, wispy grey hair, and his watery, bloodshot eyes darted everywhere as he clambered over the rail and stomped along the deck carrying his gear in a hold-all. He continually puffed out his cheeks with each breath as if he found breathing hard work.

He gave me a cursory glance and turned to climb the steps up to the first veranda beneath the bridge. Right, I thought, better get some gloves on ready for work. It looks like we'll be leaving soon.

Stepping back into the accommodation, I made my way along the alley-way and back across the catwalk to my cabin. Heat was building up from the huge boiler only two or three feet beneath me as I passed by. Then came a loud clanging from below as the telegraph rang for stand by. Speeding back from my cabin, I was confronted on the narrow catwalk by a smartly dressed figure hurrying in the opposite direction. Most Hull fishermen put to sea in their shore suits, but this man was wearing an immaculately tailored, pale blue-grey, broad pin-striped affair. This, I guessed, was the third hand, the unlicensed officer third in charge of the deck after the mate and bosun. Traditionally, he took the wheel to steer the ship out of the dock and down the Humber to the sea. This third hand, I knew, was the skipper's son. It was common knowledge in the company that Dennis Rhodes couldn't sit for his tickets because his colour vision wasn't sharp enough, so third hand was as high as he could go. Still, it was significant that he had chosen to approach the bridge via the officer's accommodation rather than over the deck.

Although Dennis was only two or three years my senior, his assured demeanour made him appear a lot older. 'Hi, Dasher! OK?' He greeted me by my nickname as we squeezed past each other. We'd never met before but he obviously knew who I was.

'Hi,' was all I could muster in reply. The noise of the auxiliary engines starting up below discouraged any further exchange.

Arriving aft, I found the mate had already chased some of the men out on deck and was leading his group forward to let go. As I approached the mess deck, some of the squad working aft with me had already left, but a couple remained lounging at one of the tables, partly supped bottles of beer in front of them. They all looked hung over to me. Thrusting my head through the doorway, I decided to chivvy them along a bit.

'Come on then, lads. Time to stand by.'

One of them gave me a baleful, red-eyed stare. 'There's enough of 'em gone already.'

'Afraid not. When the skipper rings down for stand by, he wants everyone stood by. We don't pick and choose.'

The crewman looked down at his beer. His pal looked away and a pregnant silence followed. They were thinking about it.

I didn't move.

Eventually the first man struggled to his feet. 'Come on, Ralph. I don't see the fucking point of us all being there. But we'd better go if there's gonna be a moan.'

I led the way out to the after deck. The skipper was already ordering us to take in the stern rope, and the lads laid along to pull in the long reach of the rear rope from the quay. Then came the call for the after spring. The engines began to kick us off the quay and we moved slowly back from the berth. We started off down the dock, and as usual at high water every other ship was wanting to move at the same time.

'Right then, Bosun. Where do you want this rope?' One of the men turned pointedly towards me. 'Shall we stow it in the liver house?'

Now something about this enquiry made me suspicious. Perhaps it was the way it had been made. True, the liver house was nice and handy; the doorway was right alongside the entrance to the accommodation. But the coiled ninety-foot stern rope would take up a lot of room and hamper the liver boiler in his work later in the trip. Besides this crew were regulars. They had no need to ask unless they were looking for an excuse.

'You've done a few trips in this ship, haven't you?' I said. 'What do you usually do with the rope?'

'Well,' the decky hesitated defensively, 'depends on what the bosun wants.'

'Right,' I decided quickly. 'You'd better pull it up to the boat deck then. Coil it securely between the two mooring bollards up there.'

It was a good job I knew the normal lay-out of the boat deck on all the company's ships. The lads weren't too happy dragging all that weight one deck higher, though.

I decided to ignore the mumblings of my new shipmates and concentrate instead on us squeezing past all the ships trying to back out of their berths. Crossing the stern of a Kingston ship, I spotted a similar group to ours mustered on the after deck, bosun in charge. Suddenly I heard a familiar voice. 'Know of any good dances going when we get back, Dasher?' Startled, I peered closer. It was Eddie, beaming broadly.

'Hey!' I called as we passed. '*You* didn't warn anyone you were going away, did you?'

'Snap!' he replied, as they drifted astern.

The *St Leger* was a happy enough ship, I suppose. Things were just a little too laid back for my liking, and I sensed a lack of discipline. The mate Lenny Watts was known as 'Lounging Lenny'. A slightly built five-feet seven, he hardly seemed big enough to handle the heavy work required of a mate. At every stoppage he would lounge on anything to hand while he dished out orders. Few skippers would tolerate so casual an attitude; every officer knew time was of the essence from the very start of any trip.

With such a relaxed set-up, it was no wonder the crew stayed on. They seemed to do most things to suit themselves, aided and abetted by Dennis, who naturally retained a decky's mentality. But it was bound to affect results. Dusty Rhodes seldom produced any big money trips. He just scraped by with average results, living off successes achieved during the so-called 'dip and fill' years straight after the war, from 1946 to 1948, when the grounds were at their most prolific.

On this particular trip, Dusty had chosen to head for Bear Island, the easiest of grounds from a skipper's point of view. Its gradually shelving bottom of mud and sand covered a large area right around the island and presented few snags. We enjoyed lovely, calm summer weather over most of our five days steaming and I learned more about Dusty with every watch I took on the bridge. Despite his bloodshot eyes, red nose and generally ruddy complexion, our skipper was in fact teetotal – in every sense of the word. He just couldn't get enough tea, especially once we started fishing.

The galley boy regularly humped a full enamel teapot to the bridge in the middle of each daylight watch. Even then, you'd often see the tea-pot dangling in front of your face as you walked aft along the deck. Dusty used to lower it from the bridge window on a piece of twine, bearing the plaintive message 'Please fill me'. During spells of heavy night fishing when things were hectic and everyone else fully occupied, Dusty was reduced to scurrying round and emptying the dregs from every other mug into his own. Cold and stale perhaps, it was still tea to Dusty.

When we started fishing I found out even more about the skipper. Each time the fish was cleared on any ship, the officer of the watch was expected to head for the bridge to help the skipper and learn from him, for there's a lot to consider when you're trying to catch fish to your maximum potential. The basic requirement is to keep your gear in the depth of water currently favoured by the fish, and this requires you to run the depth recorder throughout the tow, constantly marking out on paper the depth of water beneath you and thus drawing you a picture of the sea-bed.

Normally you switched the recorder off at the end of each tow – after all there's no point in running it if you're not moving – and tore the used paper away from the bottom of the machine. Dusty, however, saw no need to switch off the machine when he'd only have to turn it back on again half an hour later. So our skipper allowed the paper to flow over the bridge floor all day long. Finding a heap of curly paper spread around the sounder when I arrived on the bridge used to irritate my tidy nature, but you couldn't question the skipper.

Carrying the essential two pots of tea, I first tried stepping over the pile. But eventually I lost patience and decided to plough straight through this giant heap of tagliatelle, dragging it in long streamers across the bridge floor. Perched on his chair, Dusty said nothing. He simply frowned when he saw that the paper now covered even more of the bridge grating. Maybe he thought my efforts not to spill his tea justified my actions.

I resolved to scatter the paper ever further each time I entered the bridge. How long would the skipper stand for it before he asked us to clear it away? By the end of the day everyone else had followed my example and the foot-thick carpet of paper was fast becoming a trip hazard for anyone who didn't step warily. We could have gone on like this for days. Just how stubborn would Dusty turn out to be? But the end came suddenly. The skipper's glasses slipped off his nose and, wary of stepping on them accidentally, he asked the galley boy to clear the paper away. Only for it all to begin again, of course.

There were lots of ships in our area – anything from seventy to a hundred – all fishing within a six-mile radius, all working what was obviously a very large shoal of fish, all going in different directions, and all towing a set of gear up to a quarter of a mile astern. So on any tow you ran the risk of getting tied up with another ship's gear. The officer on the bridge was continually judging angles and distances every time he passed behind or in front of another ship, or crossed one at an angle.

Dusty's approach was to skirt round the edge of the group, picking up crumbs, until the officer of the watch came up to lend a hand or take over. Arriving on the bridge after clearing the fish off deck, I found Dusty lounging in his chair reading a magazine, making sure he kept well clear of the mêlée until help arrived. He put down his mag, then checked sounder, radar and compass, before finally pulling the wheel over towards the centre of the massive fleet of ships and setting a course through their midst. 'Steer that course as best you can. I'm just going to put my feet up in the chart-room for an hour or so.' And with that he strode off the bridge and left me to it.

I gulped and surveyed the mass of ships grouped ahead of me. Then I picked up the binoculars and started on my task of measuring distances on the radar and identifying what everyone else was doing. I was annoyed. With all his experience, this should have been the skipper's job. Still, if I wanted to learn, this was certainly an opportunity. I had little chance of following a course. I was too busy pulling the *Leger* from one side to the other just to avoid fouling other ships or their gear, and I got a bit of sweat on or found myself chewing on my muffler on a few occasions over the next hour. Eventually hauling time came round and I was only too pleased to call the skipper, who had slipped into a bit of a doze. Then I shot off the bridge and prepared to lift the gear.

When the trawl came to the surface, I'd hit the jack-pot; it laid out on the water with about 200 baskets crammed inside. I was chuffed when the four bags came aboard. It would take over two hours to gut the fish, leaving me no time to return to the bridge this tow, and forcing Dusty to get his finger out if he wanted to compete. Gutting is a back-breaking job, but the weather was fine, the sea smooth and the sun warming our backs as we towed along. I was happy gutting along with the lads and doing my job as bosun, making sure the fish were gutted clean, and that no one was dumping the more difficult types like cat-fish, which had teeth like a tiger and wriggled like an eel.

Things were going well, far too well for our job. Suddenly – wzzzz – the towing warps started pulling out. We must have come fast on the bottom. The skipper stopped the ship temporarily, but to no effect. This wasn't a fastener: someone had got our gear or vice-versa. We'd have to knock the warps out of the towing block and start hauling the gear back. The skipper did his best to manoeuvre the ship, but we couldn't heave the warps back – they just kept see-sawing in and out. Someone had definitely got hold of our gear and was pulling it in the opposite direction. But with so many ships close by, and our ship swinging around in the manoeuvres, it was difficult from the deck to tell exactly which one. The bridge windows were banging up and down – Dusty puffing and blowing as he searched with his binoculars to see who had our gear.

After some riving and pulling, the warps jumped at last and we were free of the obstruction. But when the gear came up we could see that we hadn't escaped undamaged. A couple of wires had parted and stranded, otherwise the ironwork was pretty much intact. But the net had taken a hammering: it was split right across the back of the trawl. Although a lot of fish had escaped, we still had about ninety baskets left if we could get it aboard without further mishap. We drew the fish alongside, then the mate and I hung over the rail and laced the torn edges of the trawl any old how until we could hove the fish in board.

Once the fish was in and we had spread out the trawl, we could see it was damaged all over. Men set to repairing and braiding all the way along the deck, but at least the weather remained fine. The ship was wallowing in a lazy swell and the only water coming aboard was lapping through the scupper ports. Dusty was mortified at losing fish and time. Trying to chivvy things along, he was heckling from the bridge windows and focusing most of his attention on his son, immediately below him. Dennis had landed one of the most difficult jobs, working where the wing joins the main body of the trawl and the net turns a corner, and trying to bring together both fly meshes and bosom meshes.

Dusty hung out the window. 'You're doing it wrong,' he shouted, pointing out the section where Dennis had supposedly made a mistake.

'No, I'm not,' Dennis replied. 'This is the only way I can do it.'

Pretty soon the bridge door banged and Dusty appeared on deck. Good to tell it was fine weather. He scrambled past the men working aft and came over the jumble of net, bare feet jammed into the old, unlaced boots he sometimes wore. Finishing up alongside Dennis, in what we called the duckpond, next to the biggest scupper port of the lot, he proceeded to show his son how to do the job. Water lapped in around the skipper's ankles, but he paid it no mind until the ship gave a particularly large roll and a big dollop of water swilled in right up to his knees, soaking the bottom of his trousers.

'There you are, you silly old sod,' said Dennis, the only hand who could get away with it. 'Now you'll have to go and change your pants. I can finish this off.'

Puffing and blowing even more, Dusty told Dennis what to do next. Then, still grumbling, he stomped past everyone back to the bridge. But if we thought we'd seen the last of him, we were wrong. A few minutes later he was back at the window. 'It's still not right,' he shouted, pointing down at his son.

An argument ensued. 'Of course, it's right,' Dennis replied. 'You're just looking at it from the wrong angle.'

Finally, *bang* – the bridge door went again. Out came our illustrious skipper – sporting a pair of grubby John Ls, rather baggy at the bottom, and soaking wet boots – and clumped past the grinning deckies scattered along the after deck. Dusty had clearly removed his sodden trousers when he got back to the bridge and put them on a radiator to dry, planning to go down to his cabin to fetch a fresh pair. But in the meantime he'd glanced out the window to check on Dennis, and now here he was, once again bending over his son and pointing out the error of his ways.

Suddenly a great shadow loomed over the working party. First the long fore-deck of a huge French trawler passed very close by, with two or three dozen men all working hard on a damaged set of gear, shortly followed by something like a block of flats as the vast bulk of the accommodation with its several verandas towered above us.

On the top veranda was a heavily built, thick-necked man, wearing the brass-buttoned, double-breasted uniform of a captain, albeit well-worn, complete with a crushed peaked cap rammed down over his forehead. He stood there in bulldog stance, hands turned inwards resting on the handrail, staring into our wheelhouse. Eventually, he directed his gaze towards us, a mere handful of men, gaping up at him like a cluster of chicks waiting to be fed.

'Where is the capitan?' he shouted.

We continued to stare, astounded at the sheer size of this fishing vessel. This was obviously the ship we had been tangled up with.

'*Where is the capitan?*' he roared again, square jaw thrust forward as he slowly glided past us.

Regaining his senses, Dusty pulled himself together. 'I'm the captain,' he replied, summoning all the authority he could muster.

The sea-beast looked down, visibly ducking his head for a closer look when he picked out the figure now addressing him – long underpants and boots, shirt-tail flapping, bow legs akimbo, mouth hanging open. No, his eyes had not deceived him. Smacking his hand across his forehead, he turned without a word and returned to his wheelhouse. No point in him asking what had gone wrong there. Not with a screwball in charge.

The rest of us were mortified. Heaven knows what stories would be circulating around the Frenchmen on the scene. Certainly no French trawlers came near us for the rest of the trip.

I completed a number of trips on the *St Leger* over the summer, and I viewed my time there with mixed feelings. I certainly learned a lot during my spells on the bridge: Dusty was always inclined to leave me to it and go rest his legs in the chart-room when I was up there during a tow. The *Leger* was also a happy enough ship. There were plenty of laughs – most of them down to Dusty – but I was never particularly popular. I often had to override Dennis, who was always trying to take over things that weren't his responsibility, especially when the mate was below and I was in charge of the deck. This didn't go down well at all with the third hand and his cronies, particularly as he was older than me and had more sea time.

I knew I was performing better than any other member of the crew, and that I knew more than most. But my time aboard the ship was about to come to an end in a most surprising way.

CHAPTER 4

A GREATER CHALLENGE AWAITS

Like many crews, the men of the *St Leger* got on well enough to meet up for a drink with their wives and girlfriends at the end of each trip, and anxious not to be further estranged I made sure I was part of the group. Crews usually went out on settling day, when we all got paid. But this time we had arrived home at noon and the boys decided to spend the afternoon with the girls in the St Andrew's Club.

I went home to change first. When I arrived at the club, a crowd had already gathered – men and partners crammed around three tables shoved together, with Dennis presiding at one end. Where had they got the money from? I wondered. None of us would be paid until tomorrow. Then I noticed the kitty on the table. They had all put in some cash and no one would go home until he'd had his money's worth. My contribution was duly welcomed and I joined the happy throng. These were always great times, recounting amusing incidents from past trips in front of the girls. We'd just finished the story of Dusty's Max Wall impersonation when, lo and behold, in walked the man himself, with his wife in tow.

The skipper seemed a bit surprised to see us all. The mate wasn't around, so it was Dennis who invited his mum and dad to come and join us. I was intrigued. This would certainly be a bit of a test – after all, our skipper was supposed to be teetotal. Dusty was a good sport, sitting down with us even if it was probably the last thing he wanted. He added to the kitty and ordered his drinks: a gin and tonic for his wife and a lime and lemonade for himself. He was certainly sticking to his guns so far, though I still couldn't believe his red nose and bloodshot eyes were simply down to tea. As the afternoon wore on and things got more boisterous we got through plenty of rum, whisky and beer, and Dusty had plenty of invitations to try something stronger. But he stuck with his lime and lemon and downed plenty of it.

I didn't consume as much as the others, content for the most part to sit behind a pint, spiced up with the occasional rum. My tolerance for drink has always been high, but not so Dusty's. I couldn't believe my eyes. The skipper was slowly beginning to show signs of inebriation, slurring his words and swaying along with everyone else as he knocked back his lime and lemon. Stranger still, no one had spiked his drink. I was confident of that because I was watching out for it.

I wasn't the only one who had noticed what was happening. Some of the women were also looking at Dusty, ever more flushed as he giggled away at our silly jokes and copied the antics of the drunken deckies around him. People drifted in and out of the club, and I was just thinking it was time I made my excuses, when in walked Eddie Woolford. He grinned when he spotted me, gave me the thumbs up and nodded towards the bar. I hadn't seen Eddie since we'd both missed the student dance, so I got up and followed him over. There he met up with a young fisherman who was a stranger to me.

'Hi, Rob,' Eddie greeted me. 'Haven't seen you for a while.'

'No, not since we missed out on that student do.'

'You're right. Well, we've a chance to make up for that. Meet Ralph. He sails for Hellyer's and his girlfriend's a student. He's meeting her and a few of her pals at the Gardener's Arms, up near the university. He says we can go along.'

'Hi, Ralph.' I leant across and shook his hand. 'Hope you don't mind us tagging on.'

'Not at all,' he replied. 'You can keep some of the others occupied while I get to close quarters with Hanna.'

'You'll enjoy it,' Eddie chipped in. 'I've been a couple of times before and it's rocking. There are some pretty girls too – if you can get past the men. But some bottles of beer to take out should do for that.'

The barman took our orders, all of us asking for shorts for a bit of Dutch courage, and pretty soon Ralph's taxi arrived. The lads set off towards the door, while I went back to finish off my drink and say cheerio. As I moved down the table, Dusty suddenly stuck out his hand. 'I'll say best of luck then, Dash,' he said cheerily, 'since you won't be going back next trip.'

This was news to me. 'Whyever not?' I replied

'Better not discuss it now.' The skipper dismissed me with a wave of the hand. 'You'll find out tomorrow.'

I drifted out through the door towards the taxi, my mind all over the place. What on earth could he be talking about?

'Come on, Bob,' called Eddie from the back of the car. 'We're wasting time. Don't want to be beaten to the snatch again.'

Ralph giggled. Temporarily dismissing Dusty Rhodes from my mind, I climbed into the front seat of the taxi and away we roared to the other side of town.

The Gardener's Arms was a large country-style pub, even though the surrounding area had long since been developed. A large bar circled through the Smoke Room and the Lounge, and it also had a Snug. All three rooms were busy, mostly with students from the university just up the road. Our contact Ralph led the way to the bar, nodding to one or two young chaps as he went along, but he couldn't spot his so-called girlfriend so we decided to move to the bar, get a drink and search the other rooms. We each ordered a half of Hull Brewery mild and took our glasses through to the next room. And there our luck was about to turn.

Ralph's friend Hanna was sitting with three friends – Amy, Jenny and John. They appeared to be quite merry already and greeted us cheerfully as Ralph introduced us to Hanna, who in turn introduced us to the others. Jenny was a pretty girl with a perpetual smirk, while Amy had specs and crooked teeth but laughed and giggled a lot. John meanwhile seemed easy-going enough; I reckon he just liked hanging around with the girls. We quickly squeezed in around the table and did what was undoubtedly expected of us, that is order a round of drinks. Like most others, students thought fishermen were both wealthy and generous.

Looking around, I could see the attraction of students. Apart from the sheer number of pretty girls, they had a relaxed and zany attitude and some were dressed weirdly, with exaggerated ear-rings and jewellery, even streaks of colour in their hair. I studied the two girls opposite us. Jenny was slim and attractive, but that smirk made her seem far too self-assured. She looked like a girl who would always want to call the tune. Amy was no oil painting but obviously fun to be with, though I'm not sure either would have been my choice. Happily, when time was called at three o'clock, we got the chance to broaden the field.

'If you want to meet some more of our friends, why not get a couple of bottles of wine and bring them back to our house,' said Amy. 'We've got a record player and we could put some of the latest hits on.'

This seemed to suit everyone, though my two mates wrinkled their noses at the thought of wine. I expected they would manage to include a couple of bottles of Moors' & Robson's mild.

'Don't worry, boys,' muttered Ralph. 'Hanna says there'll be one or two sexy girls at Amy's place. Apparently Angelica's the one to look out for. Her mother's French.'

This time the usual taxi wasn't required as Amy's block was within walking distance, only a couple of hundred yards away. She led us to a row of large Victorian houses, each three stories high, plus attics in the roof. As we climbed the three stone steps to the large, panelled front door, Rosemary Clooney was on again, this time singing 'This Ole House'. We entered a wide hall-cum-passageway. A broad flight of stairs rose up on the left, while to the right a passage ran through to a scullery and beyond to an old wash-house. Two doors led off the right-hand side of this passage, the music blasting from the wide-open door of the second.

'This is our common-room,' said Hanna, as the three girls led the way. The large room had a bay window looking out over a dismal back yard. A couple of unmatched, sagging leather sofas provided the seating, while the electric record player and a scattering of seventy-eights stood on a tired-looking chest of drawers. A lad was jiving away with three or four girls, but over by the chimney-breast a very slim young lady was lounging on one of the sofas. With one arm draped over the back of the sofa, and a half-filled tumbler in her hand, she immediately drew the eye. Her dark, raggy hair hung down below her shoulders and had a nice sheen to it, while her shapely top lip curved up somewhat, revealing front teeth which she constantly tickled with her tongue. Her short dress showed plenty of thigh and she looked very sexy in an elfin sort of way. She also looked bored.

The boys and I brought the booze into the room and placed it on the table in the bay window. I was carrying one of the bottles of wine, so I decided to approach the femme fatale on the couch and offer her a refill. She cast an appraising eye over me as I came closer.

'Would you like that glass topping up a bit?' I asked loudly over the music.

She paused and gave me a pointed look. 'Those pants don't suit you,' she stated boldly. 'Why don't you take them off?'

'What, now?'

'Why not?'

'Why don't you take yours off instead?' I grinned at her.

'I'm not wearing any,' she replied coolly.

She made no effort to back up her claim, but studying the glint in her eye and the way she was running her tongue back and forth over those lovely white teeth, I knew she was telling the truth. She wanted to get me to challenge her, but I wasn't going to rise to the bait.

'You must be Angelica,' I said.

'Oh, so my fame's gone before me, has it?'

'Not really,' I tried to reassure her. 'It's just the girls said you'd be here and I thought the name fitted.'

'Oh, so you think I look angelic, do you?' In the background Jim Reeves was singing 'I Fall to Pieces.'

'Sure,' I hesitated, struggling to cover my indiscretion 'Well, in some ways, certainly.'

Putting her drink down on the floor, Angelica suddenly jumped up and advanced towards me. 'This is a slower one. Let's dance together for a while.'

As she closed with me, she pushed me towards the other dancers and wrapped her arms around my bottom, swaying to the music and pulling me tight to her pelvis. Angelica was hot stuff, all right. And her smouldering eyes suggested she was in the mood for satisfaction. Glancing up, I spotted Eddie over by the table in the window. Drink in hand, he was talking to another of the new girls. But he was still watching me, pursing his lips and giving me the thumbs up when he caught my eye.

The music stopped. Time to cool things off a bit, I thought. Angie and her wandering hands looked like trouble to me. 'Where's the lavatory?' I asked.

'In the wash-house through the back.'

Excusing myself, I hurried out of the room, through the scullery and out to the concrete-floored wash-house. A latched, green-painted plank door opened outwards to reveal a porcelain bowl with overhead tank and chain, just like you'd find in the back yards of most of the terraced houses on the south side of Hessle Road. I stepped inside, pulled the door shut and started to relieve myself. But suddenly the door opened again and in came Angie. Startled, I had to stop in midstream and cover myself quickly.

'Just thought you might need some help.' She grinned up at me, reaching for my crotch.

'Look, Angie,' I said, grabbing her by both wrists and giving her my most winning smile. 'There's something you've got to realise. The penis is designed for two purposes but it can't perform them both at the same time. I don't want to be anywhere we can be disturbed. You go back till I've finished off here and I'll come and find you.'

I was bending over her as I spoke. She jumped up and gave me a peck on the lips, then turned and left. I was chuffed at this show of affection. Angie really did fancy me. It wasn't just lust after all.

Back in the hallway, I found her sitting on the fourth step of the staircase. The door to the common-room was closed.

'Hello! Had enough?'

'What do you mean, enough?' Her eyes were twinkling. 'I haven't had any yet?' She opened and closed her knees, giving me tantalising glimpses that she was indeed knickerless. 'Come on, I'll show you my flat.'

Extending her hand, she led me up to the first floor. The flat turned out to be a large, bay-windowed front bedroom overlooking the main road. The furniture had all seen better days: a double mattress on an old-fashioned, brass-knobbed metal bed-frame, a large polished maple-wood wardrobe in one corner, a well-worn easy chair in the window, and a small kitchen table with chair and stool, a kitchen sink and a cooker against the back wall. 'What do you think?' asked Angelica, closing the door behind me with one hand while gesturing grandly with other. 'It may not be much but the bed's very comfy.'

Grabbing my arm, Angie pulled me towards the bed in question, spun me round and pushed me flat, giving me no time to recover before she launched herself spread-eagled on top of me and knocked the wind out of us both. 'Oh, I do love big men,' she panted. Placing her cheek close to mine, she stretched up and began to nuzzle my neck and nibble my ear. Sliding off to one side, she undid the middle button of my shirt, worked her hand inside and began massaging my chest. Seconds later she was heading down below my waistband. Hey up! I thought. What's going on here? Seduction was my job.

Unused to women taking the initiative, I slid my hand gently up Angie's thigh, but just as I reached the garden of excitement she jumped up again. Quickly unfastening my waistband, she grabbed the bottom of my trouser legs and began tugging them down. I started to giggle. 'Hey, be careful,' I pleaded, as she rived my pants back and forth like a dog. 'You'll tear them.'

Eventually, with much laughter all round, the trousers came off, followed in short order by my underpants. Then Angie took charge of the union of our private parts. She mounted me and began to bounce and gyrate, the glazed look in her eyes betraying nothing but satisfaction and relief. Her breath came ever more quickly and I knew I wouldn't last long. Her lustful antics had long since aroused me and being fully dressed up top but completely naked down below made the act even more erotic. Pretty soon we were both spent.

Angie slid off me like an exhausted jockey. She lay by my side for a while, a tired smile of conquest playing around her lips. Then she started up once more, showing a bit more affection this time, no doubt hoping to arouse me again. We spent the next hour or so like this, titillating, exciting and satisfying each other. Now it was time for a change. 'Let's go get something to eat,' I suggested.

'No, let me get something for you,' said Angie. 'I can cook you know.' And off she went to cook me cheese and scrambled egg on toast.

It wasn't the full-blown meal I had in mind but I didn't want to offend her. She made another helping and topped it off with coffee and buns. As the evening wore on, she even produced a quarter bottle of sherry her mother had shared with her. That was followed by another gift from her mother: a diaphanous little nightie. 'Mother said I should save this for my first real boyfriend,' purred Angie. She put it on, posing and cavorting so sensuously that another session in bed was the inevitable result.

Eventually sleep overtook us and I awoke next morning full of guilt. I hadn't warned my mother I was going to stay with friends and I'd been out all night! And today was settling day. Not only did I have to collect my money, I had to find out what Dusty had been on about. Angie was already starting to fondle me again, but I needed a shower and a change of clothes. Shipmates had always suggested that meeting up with a 'Nympho' was heaven, but I'd discovered the hard way that it could be pretty wearing too.

Settling time at the company office was normally about eleven o'clock, but I had to get home first, and I was the wrong side of town with very little money left in hand. Angie was in no hurry to get up, even though she had a lecture at ten, clinging to me like a kitten to its mum when I tried to do so. Reluctantly, she told me there was a taxi office round the corner and made me promise to meet up with her that night. A smoochy kiss and off I went.

Like any good fisherman, I kept the taxi waiting half an hour while I showered and changed. It was just gone eleven by the time I got to the company yard, but they'd started settling early and most of the crew had already been and gone. Significantly, the hopefuls still hanging around in search of a ship included a chap called Dodsley – an experienced bosun, I knew.

Suspicion etched across my face, I entered the runner's office, challenging Jack Gibby as soon as I got inside. 'What's going on, Jack? Am I going back or what?'

'I don't think so,' he replied guardedly.

'Whyever not? Has Dusty asked for a change? What's he had to say?'

'Just hang on there, Bob.' Gibby held up his hands. 'You've got to go and see your old man. I'll phone up and let him know you're here.'

'The old man,' I repeated, frowning. 'What on earth has he got to do with it?'

As the firm's ship's husband and outside manager, my father had overall responsibility for ensuring our vessels were re-stored and refurbished after each trip. It was also his job to look after the skippers. Generally speaking, he concerned himself with the crews from bosun down only if there was a problem.

'He's here,' said Gibby tersely into the phone. 'Send him right up, OK.'

Replacing the handset, Gibby jerked his thumb upwards. I knew he would tell me nothing more.

Mounting the stairs leading up from the front door of the company offices was not a new experience for me. Normally I would turn right towards the accountant's pay windows, but now I headed left instead and approached the door to the manager's office. I knocked lightly on its frosted-glass window. 'Come in,' barked a familiar voice. I entered the room and closed the door behind me.

The office was large, with a bay window looking right over the first of the two fish docks. My father was sitting in a well-upholstered swivel chair behind a large, square, leather-topped desk, covered with the usual paper trays, telephones, loose papers and such. Over by the window, a small, ferret-like man was reclining in a comfortable, high-backed easy chair. His hooked nose and lively eyes were prominent in a weather-beaten face. I recognised him vaguely as one of the older skippers, new to our company even though he'd been around for some time.

'Now, Rob,' said my father, gesturing towards the captain. 'You know Skipper Alf Farguson, don't you?'

'Yes, of course.' I nodded towards him as I spoke. 'How'd you do, Skipper?'

'Skipper Farguson is looking to take you on as mate!' My father watched me closely as he dropped this bombshell. 'Alf wants to train you up to his way of working. I'm not sure you're ready but he reckons you are. What do you think?'

His way of working, I had no illusions about that. Alf Farguson was one of the old school. He had worked as a decky before the introduction of watches below, when men stayed on deck for days at a time until they'd either filled the ship or collapsed with exhaustion. Ships *were* much smaller then and quicker to fill, but he would offer no respite to the man who ran the deck, and expect nothing less than maximum effort. On the other hand, Alf had been one of Hull's most successful skippers for years. His knowledge of the grounds was unsurpassed and I could learn a lot from him.

My answer had to be quick and decisive. 'Yes, I think I'm ready enough. I'll do a good job for the skipper, with a little guidance from him.'

'Sure you're ready,' Alf was already interrupting me. 'I'll soon lick you into shape.'

'Well, that's decided then,' said the old man. 'Better go and sign on. She's sailing early tomorrow morning.'

I floated downstairs and up the yard to the runner's office. Gibby was lounging with one arm on his desk, a knowing look in his eye. Behind him, his mate Benny looked up from the papers in front of him and smiled.

'What news?' asked Gibby.

'I'm going mate with Fargy.' The words came tumbling out.

'Well, there you are then,' he said, grinning. 'He's a bit eccentric but you'll earn some cash. So Dusty didn't fire you after all. Here, you'd better sign off and sign on the *Keverne*.'

After settling and completing my other business at the office, I dashed off on to Hessle Road to get the extra stores I would need in my new position, including my own marlin spike for splicing warps. It was going to be a mad rush. I only had the rest of the day to get everything done, packing included, and my mother knew nothing about my promotion yet. No doubt she'd worry when she learned about my extra responsibilities. And how could she possibly get my three changes of clothing washed and dried in time for this quick turn round? I'd obviously have to go buy extra at Tiplady's, the fishermen's outfitter.

I also had to get the bag man to shift the great oilskin bag containing my heavy waterproofs and thigh-boots (which normally remained on board between trips) from the bosun's berth on the *St Leger* to the mate's berth on the *St Keverne*. It would cost me five shillings, a fair amount. But it would be money well earned humping that big bag out of one narrow accommodation and into another, and possibly over a few ship's decks as well.

At the end of the working day we all sat down to the evening meal at home. There was much excitement at my early promotion, though my mother and my sister were both anxious. They weren't sure if I would be strong enough to cope, particularly after my father pointed out that I was taking on the toughest job on the deck. Two years ago, the surgeon had told me that I'd never be able to return to sea, but I'd proved him wrong already and I hoped to do so again.

Now the evening lay before me. I'd only spent one night at home (well, ashore anyway!) and wanted to take my last chance to relax. Angelica and I had already agreed to meet again that evening in the Gardener's Arms, and everything was ready for my departure between one and two in the morning. All that remained now was to enjoy the rest of the night. It would take me two buses to cross town so, with money in my pocket and time of the essence, I called a taxi.

Back at the Gardener's, I soon found Angie in the same room with the same group of friends, among them Ralph, the fisher lad who had introduced us all. Angie's face lit up when she saw me and she gestured for me to take the seat next to her. 'I'm glad you got here early, Bob.' She grabbed my arm as I sat down. 'We're all going to the dance at Beverley Road baths. Then when it's finished you and I can go back to my place.' She hunched her shoulders in gleeful anticipation.

'Whoa, just a minute, Angie.' I tried to rein in her racing imagination. 'I won't be going back anywhere. In fact, I might not be able to stay till the end of the dance.'

'What do you mean?' She looked crestfallen.

'Well, I'm sailing on a new ship early in the morning. I might have to leave before midnight.'

'Oh, Bob. That's awful. I was hoping to have you to myself for a while. But I don't want to miss the dance. I was really looking forward to dancing with a big fellow like you.'

'There's no need for us to miss it. Let's have some fun while we can.'

'We will,' she replied with a wink. 'Don't worry, I'll make sure of that.'

The nearby baths often put on dances in the evening and the gang were in ebullient mood as we made our way over there. We paid our fee at the door and paused at the cloakroom while the girls hung their coats on one of several racks. There was no ticket or attendant but we figured the coats would be safe enough. Things were pretty lively in the main dance hall and it was already quite full. A local band, Harry Chatterton and his Modernairs, was blasting it out, and Angelica soon had me out on the floor doing some sort of jive or jitterbug, though when the opportunity presented itself she also seized the chance to hold me close and cling tight.

Of course, we all paid plenty of visits to the bar, and these went on longer and longer as the night progressed, eventually leaving Angie and me alone at a large round table. Angie grabbed hold of my hand underneath the table, sliding it under her dress and up her inner thigh. Once again she was wearing no knickers. Then, giggling, she thrust my hand away. I was starting to watch the time. I certainly didn't want to leave it too late before ordering a taxi to take me down the dock. Catching on fast, Angie suddenly grabbed me by the arm again. 'Come with me,' she ordered, dragging me out to the cloakroom.

'Hang on a minute.' I was wondering what she was up to. 'I can order a cab from the ticket office before we go.'

'I know but we're not leaving yet.'

She led me through the by now crowded racks of coats straight to the back of the room, eventually stopping next to a radiator topped by a shelf. Turning towards me with a sultry look in her eyes, she put her hand behind my head and stretched up towards me. Then, smouldering eyes half-closed and lips pursed, she closed with me in a complete top-to-toe engagement. As we enveloped each other, swaying slightly to the distant music, her other hand reached down and started massaging my crotch. So sensual were her movements that they quickly achieved the desired effect and she began to undo my fly. Thank God it was one of the new zip type and not a buttoned affair – I might have to retrieve things quickly later on.

Now she hitched herself up on to the shelf, tucked her dress up, spread her legs and pulled me towards her.

The sight of her slim, shapely body, and of those generous milky thighs as they guided me into her shady cavern of ecstasy, made my left knee tremble as I reached up towards her. Overwhelmed both by the sensation of entering her and by the effort I was putting in, I was gasping for breath as I strove to maximise our union, stretching and scrabbling like a dog in the street ... At the same time Angie was rocking backwards and forwards on the edge of the shelf as if she was riding a walking horse ... The excitement was building when ... we heard voices approaching. The coat-racks hid us to some extent, but our heavy breathing would definitely betray us if someone came right into the room.

Clearly excited by the risk of discovery, Angie climaxed quickly and her early orgasm brought me on as well. And a good job too, I thought, though for the moment the voices remained outside. My breathing soon returned to normal and we quickly composed ourselves, moving along the racks and grabbing our coats just as the newcomers came in.

When I went to order a taxi, I found one was already waiting outside. I wanted Angie to stay with her friends, but she was having none of it, even though I had to go home first for my kit-bag. I insisted she keep her head down when we got there, making it in and out of the house in five minutes flat. Angie was particularly amorous throughout the trip, writhing and groping in the back of the cab, and things would soon have got out of hand had I not been so firm with her.

Fishermen consider it bad luck for women to see them off at the quayside – something I made quite clear to Angie on the journey down. 'On no account must you get out of the cab when we get to the dock,' I told her. But before I knew it we were already at the *St Keverne* and the driver was putting me down right alongside my new ship. I was early, but the decks were already brightly lit and one of the bridge windows was standing open. And was that a pair of beady eyes I could see peeping over the sill?

I said goodbye to Angie with a couple of smoochy kisses, opened the door, slung out my kit-bag and followed it as quickly as possible, slamming the door behind me. I paid off the driver ... and out jumped Angie, almost devouring me as she flung her arms around me – just what I needed with the captain looking on. I disengaged myself rapidly and legged it for the safety of the ship.

CHAPTER 5

SECOND IN COMMAND

Once aboard, I made my way to my berth amidships, two decks below the bridge and directly beneath the skipper's cabin. I spent a few minutes sorting out my gear and laying out my mattress in the new bunk, though I knew the skipper would be expecting me on the bridge pretty soon. No doubt he'd berate me about the manner of my arrival. I could have kept out of his way for a while had I still been a bosun, but as second in command I had to report for orders.

Still, I went aft first to check the calibre of my crew and find out what sort of state they were in. Bringing a crew into line was always difficult when we sailed this late at night. Like me, they would have been enjoying themselves right up to the last minute in the pubs and clubs, without showing quite the same amount of restraint where drink was concerned. A quick spin around the mess deck, galley and accommodation would soon show me what was what. How many drunks would I be facing? And how many men could I rely on? To my surprise, a lot of the faces were unknown to me. Odd when I'd sailed for so many years with this company. Then light dawned; most of the crew would be Alf Fargy's regulars, having transferred with him from their previous firm. No bad thing from my point of view. At least they'd have no preconceptions about me.

With one or two exceptions, the crew were all aboard and I finally made my way to the bridge to face the old man. I arrived to find Alf chuntering at the wireless operator. Apparently the picture on the radar screen wasn't good enough. Fancy the sparks making himself available so early in the proceedings, I thought to myself. But he was hardly likely to be a volunteer. Since he needed to be close to the wireless room, his cabin was on the same deck as that of the captain. I bet Alf had given him no chance to settle in and had dragged him out of his berth early to get things sorted. That just goes to show how much drive our skipper had; he was a little terrier.

Fargy certainly didn't miss the opportunity to lay into me over Angie's amorous farewell. But hardly was he into his stride before Benny arrived and saved my bacon. 'The crew's all aboard,' he reported. Everything's ready to go.'

That was good enough for Alf, anxious as always to avoid the queue of ships waiting to leave the dock. 'Have the crew stand by,' he ordered me. Then he rang the signal to the engineers.

I left quickly by the wing door, scampering down the ladder from the veranda and across the engine-room casing top. The crew had been pretty boozed up when I left them. What sort of response would I receive when I turned them out? In the event there were no problems. I didn't even have to divide them fore and aft; they just sorted themselves out. Leaving the lock, I proudly took up the mate's traditional position right forward on the top of the fo'c'sle head, my new status easily identifiable to the handful of by-standers on the dock side. From here, bang in the eyes of the ship, with sight-lines clear up and down the river, I could warn the skipper of any approaching danger.

As we cleared the dock, a sharp-faced, wiry decky stepped towards me from a group sorting out the head rope. 'Just thought I'd let you know, Mr Mate, I'm the fish-room man in this ship,' He stared up at me, glassy eyed, 'I've made a few trips with this skipper as fish-room man now.'

Now this was a surprise. The mate normally selected his own fish-room man, the decky who took charge of preserving the catch while the mate was on the bridge. The job was a tough one. No heavy lifting was involved, but the fish-room man required stamina and determination, as well as the ability to react quickly when the fish came pouring down the hatch. He also had to be trustworthy. After all, the mate was ultimately responsible for the condition of the fish brought to market, and he would be judged by the owners on his performance. I was keen to put into practice the lessons I'd learned on the *St Dominic* and I needed someone who would follow my instructions. Knowing little of the crew and their capabilities, I decided to give this guy a chance. He looked nippy enough, and energetic too.

'What's your name?' I asked him.

'Harry, Harry Petch.'

'OK, Harry. We'll see how you do. In the meantime though, have a look under the anchor windlass for the anchor pipe cap, then secure it well with a piece of tarpaulin to keep the water out.' And with that, I turned and left the fo'c'sle head. The rest of the crew knew what they needed to do to clear up the deck and secure for sea, and organising them was the bosun's job anyway; I'd moved beyond that now. As we sailed down the river, my place was on the bridge with the skipper. The job I'd given Harry was an awkward one and would provide a good test of his competence.

We were bound for Iceland this trip, little more than three days away, so there was no time to waste to get everything ready for fishing – and that *was* my responsibility. First we had to drag the trawl out of the hold and put it alongside the ship, securing it to the ground rope and shackling it to the towing wires. Then we had to prepare the big trawl doors with their wires. We also had the spare trawls to make ready, the derricks to bring down into position and the fish-room to organise. It would be a shambles down there, with thousands of newly washed fish-boards all in a heap. I'd have to make sure there was no slacking when I wasn't around to supervise.

I took the first watch till breakfast at seven-thirty. I wasn't due back until tea-time but I knew I'd be out and about again long before that. The bosun, Joe Tompkins, took the next watch, which would last until dinner at noon. Joe was a large, podgy man, pale and flabby of face. He was placid enough, but his perpetual know-it-all smirk made him seem untrustworthy to me. I suspected he was what we called a back-biter, criticising me behind my back when I was out of earshot. Still, he was happy enough to follow my instructions for now. He would clear away any essential new stores from the hold hatchway and prepare the working trawl for lifting on deck. Then I would turn out to take over again.

I turned in after breakfast at eight o'clock and was out again less than four hours later, anxious to find the bosun before he went off watch. Joe was busy putting two Gilson wires down the forehold hatch, preparing to heave out the trawl. What an appalling sight it was! The trawl ear-marked for our trip was old and completely chafed out, the net dried out and flimsy, liable to break under any kind of strain. It looked like we'd be repairing between every haul. The tight old devil, this job was going to be extra tough.

By the time we'd eased the trawl past all the obstacles on deck, it was second sitting for dinner and Joe was due to turn in. The third hand, a little Fleetwood chap called Barry Winn, would take the next watch. As third hand, Barry couldn't take responsibility for putting the trawl alongside, but he could still get some squaring out done. Meanwhile I would get some extra gear on and then go down with the bosun for a quick bite to eat. But I never got the chance to finish my meal. Hardly had I sat down before the old man sent word that he had another job for me. It was time to hand out the duty-free stores and other goodies to the crew.

Fargy's order came as no surprise to me – although the skipper bought in the stores and the duty-free allowance, dishing them out was normally reserved for the mate and the sparks – but it did give me a problem. Even though I was working extra time I just wasn't getting to the deck work, and now I'd have to go fetch the stores from the skipper's cabin (and from the bond locker for the duty-free) and distribute them. 'Can you give me an extra hour on deck?' I asked the bosun. 'We've got to make sure the trawl's positioned properly. Then the rest of the day crew can carry on until I get back.'

Joe agreed, if grudgingly, and as it turned out I needn't have asked. Barry had spent a couple of years with Alf Fargy and knew exactly how the skipper liked his trawls fixed.

I took the sparks and a few of the off-duty lads to the skipper's berth to hump all the boxes down to the officers' mess, picking up the list of stores from the old man on the way. We would need it to work out each man's ration. A mixture of goodies accompanied the usual baccy and cigs, among them chocolate bars, soap, six bottles of beer per man and, most unusually, a crate of eggs. Few owners put eggs on board, figuring we got enough protein from the fish we ate three times a day. And few skippers would bother with them either: too fragile, too likely to lose them money.

'What do you want me to do with these?' I asked old Alf. 'Put them in the cook's store?'

'Certainly not,' he snapped. 'Last trip they asked me for eggs so I've ordered twenty dozen. Give 'em a dozen each. They can look after them themselves. Our cook does make very good pastry, though. So I've promised him a dozen as well to give the lads a treat.'

'But that makes twenty-one shares,' I said, aghast. 'We can't have a dozen each. Shall I give the surplus to the cook as well?'

'No, I won't pay for any more than a dozen for him,' snorted the skipper, sticking out his jaw.

'Couldn't we all share the cost of the extra?'

'No, I won't have the lads accusing me of fiddling them out of anything. Straight as a die I am. Share everything out equal.'

'But that works out to something like eleven and a half each.' I started feverishly on the arithmetic. 'How on earth do I give 'em half an egg each?'

'Leave it to them. They'll figure it out. Now off you go. They're all waiting for a smoke.'

I tumbled down the ladder to the deck below. The sparks was already ripping open boxes, spreading out their contents on and around the table, while the crewmen waited in the alley-way with their pillowcases. 'Leave that to me, Len,' I told him. 'You take this list and work out how much we can issue each man. And see if you can find a way of dividing twenty dozen eggs into twenty-one equal shares.'

'Can't be done, can it?' drawled the experienced RO. 'You're gonna finish up with part of an egg each. Where are we going to keep these eggs anyway? They'll soon get tossed about.'

'Don't ask me. The old man's adamant.'

'Playing silly buggers again, eh?'

'He just said to let them sort it. We just tell 'em what they're due. Come on, we'll take the first one, if you're ready.'

Most of the time you could issue comfort supplies quite quickly, particularly when the majority of the crew had already agreed on the stores. The men would let you know what tobacco or cigs they wanted, and you might have to ask about one or two other items, but that was it. On my command, the first in line stepped into the little mess and held out a pillowcase for his tobacco and cig papers. Then he stood quietly while I counted out his share of the other goodies. Finally, I shoved into his hands a tray of eggs, minus one.

'Do I have to take these?' He looked up at me quizzically.

'Yep,' I replied tersely, 'and you've another half egg to come. Next!'

Bewildered, the decky staggered off down the alley-way, balancing the eggs on one arm.

'Where did this guy come from?' I could hear him saying to the queue outside. 'He's only trying to dish out half a fucking egg to every man.'

Oh dear, this wasn't going to do much for my credibility.

Eventually every man had received his allocation, with many an argument over where to keep this unexpected bounty. Understandable really – most of the crewmen had lockers no bigger than lockers at the baths, and they were meant to keep all their spare gear in there, including kit-bags. I returned the remaining stores, plus list, to the skipper and returned to the important work on deck. But that wasn't the end of my problems. The old man called me up again. 'There's a packet of cig papers missing,' he said. 'Find out what's happened to it.'

I checked and double-checked, but all to no avail. Eventually I offered to replace the missing packet with one of my own. But Alf was having none of it. 'I'll rob no man,' he insisted. At length, I said I'd go and check the empty boxes awaiting disposal on the deck below. I couldn't believe the fuss he was making over one threepenny packet of cig papers. After a cursory look round, I nipped into my berth, grabbed a packet of papers from my share, returned to the captain's cabin and flourished the lost item.

'I've found 'em,' I said. 'They were under a flap in the bottom of a cardboard box.'

Not good enough – Fargy had now located the elusive packet himself.

'Don't try that trick again,' he told me in no uncertain terms. 'I'll rob no man and no man'll rob me.'

I'd always suspected that Fargy would be pedantic. What I hadn't realised was that he would also be so obsessive and, as I was soon to find out, pretty vicious too.

The fine weather helped us with our preparations, and we had some extra time as Alf was heading for the north side of Iceland. On the fourth day out, I reported to our captain towards the end of my watch. 'Everything's ready,' I told him.

'OK.' Alf seemed unconcerned. 'What arrangements have you made to prevent boarding?'

This was a puzzle. 'What do you mean?' I asked.

'Surely you've not forgotten?' Alf replied. Iceland extended the limit from four miles to twelve last year. Their gunboat could well try and board us if we get in close, port side probably, while we're hauling.'

This was something I hadn't considered. As one of the old-style skippers, a lot of Fargy's favourite grounds would be inside the new unilaterally imposed limit-line.

'OK, I'll work something out,' I said unconvincingly.

The bosun and third hand had one or two ideas – already employed, or so they said, by other ships – and we came up with some others ourselves. So as each of us came on watch we started to get stuff together to hang outboard along the rail. Although Fargy didn't use the port gear, we decided to lower the derricks fore and aft on that side and swing them outboard to deter any gunboat from coming too close. Then we stretched a wire between the two derricks, lining it with metal floats to drop on any small boat attempting to board. Fargy seemed satisfied: none of our measures would stop determined navy men, but they might slow them down enough for us to man the battlements.

Steaming out to the furthest point of Iceland, our skipper started fishing off the North Cape, where a smattering of ships were already searching the large Stranda Grund and taking smallish catches of thirty or forty baskets a time – still not bad for quality fish. Fargy chose to try the eastern edge of the flat first, towing down what my father and many old skippers called the Fairy River, a gully running along the edge of the bank towards the coast. But spotting the new limit-line was a problem. The old line lay four miles offshore as measured from a baseline drawn straight from headland to headland, and experienced men knew when they were drawing close by placing one mountain peak behind another. But with the new twelve-mile limit this was no longer possible. The radar gave a very poor picture of the land, and by the time you'd lined up the mountains you were already inside the line.

Alf decided to ignore it for the time being. Shooting away on the eastern edge, we hauled sixty to seventy baskets, mostly cod and haddock – prime, lively, shiny, quality fish. I was looking forward to implementing my theories regarding its storage. But would my new fish-room man Harry be up to the task?

The weather remained pretty good, but the fish was proving elusive, giving us no more than a few hauls in any one spot. We worked our way right across the north coast of Iceland, ending up off the east coast, off Telegraph Bank, so called from the telegraph wire that ran across it. Harry had been working reasonably well throughout this time. Even though my methods meant extra work for him, laying out the fish by hand in the pounds, for the most part he had followed my orders. There was just one problem: Harry wouldn't stop running to the old man and tattling about the fish-room. And whenever the skipper asked how much fish we had on board, Harry always exaggerated the amount. I'd never heard of a fish-room man undermining a mate like this before, and I had to warn him repeatedly about his conduct.

Fortunately, the way I was controlling the deck met with the skipper's approval. We were hauling and shooting the gear quickly enough for him – something of an achievement given his critical nature – and my knowledge of net construction and organisation of its speedy repair had impressed both skipper and bosun alike. So all in all I was doing OK and quickly gaining in confidence.

Our time on the fishing grounds was limited – always the case when you're dealing with fresh fish – and the days were slipping by. The odd bit of net damage apart, we were doing all right on Telegraph Bank, fishing on our own, pretty close to the old four-mile limit, but inside Iceland's newly declared extension. One afternoon I was in the middle of sorting out some damage to the trawl when the skipper suddenly shouted for the crew. A gunboat was approaching. 'Get on the port side' he cried.

I reacted immediately, ordering all hands to follow the skipper's orders and keep an eye on the intruder, while the decky learner and I carried on with the repairs. The Icelandic gunboats had already made themselves known several times during the trip. They would pick out a vessel inside the limit, cruise alongside and hail it over the loudspeaker. But Alf was more agitated on this occasion, insisting I get across to the port side straight away and take charge. On my arrival I could see why: a Z boat was edging towards us carrying five seamen, some of them – by the look of it – armed. The lads had all picked up crowbars and hatch battens and were banging them on the ship's rail. Worryingly, one man even had an axe.

The small boat stood off, about twenty yards away, and started to deliver its spiel. Meanwhile a couple of the lads disappeared aft, returning with armfuls of potatoes which they began throwing at our adversaries. One of the men in the Z boat brandished his gun, but that was the end of it. The officer-in-charge ordered a return to the gunboat and the immediate threat was over. We returned to our repairs, paying away the gear as soon as we could. Fargy streamed it off and we headed away from the contentious twelve-mile limit.

By now it was nearly time to head for home. I felt I'd won the respect of most of the crew – I had treated them in a firm but humorous fashion and my mistakes had been few. Our skipper, however, was a different matter. We barely had a passable trip on board, despite Harry's attempts to boost my figures, and Fargy was very crotchety. The extra effort demanded of a mate, patrolling and controlling every part of the deck, had taxed me to the full, and I was always grateful for my watch below – providing, that is, I could actually enjoy it. The skipper often called me out again for some triviality or other, and on our last day I turned out to find us half way through hauling.

'We didn't catch anything last haul,' said the decky who called me. We pulled in the belly – the bag was going to be a big one – only to see that the trawl was clearly split on top, the result no doubt of the gunboat chasing us out into fouler ground. It would be difficult to hove the bag in, but we had a wire becket to help with big bags and I decided to use it. As I was slinging the bag on the becket, Alf appeared at the bridge window. 'Isn't the bag a bit too big for that?' he wittered.

'It's sixty to seventy baskets,' I replied. 'We've hove in seventy before.' And I continued to sling the bag, hanging the becket on the large, double-purchase tackle wire. Then we began heaving the net along the rail towards the forr'ard fish-pounds while I followed it, eyes fixed on the lift. The tackle was taking the weight well enough, though the double net of the cod-end was stretched rather taut. But just as the bulk of the bag reached the top of the rail, the net started to tear and the fish began to pour out. I raised my hand. Heave faster, I signed to the winchman. We had to get the fish inboard before any more got away.

The skipper squawked and a decky behind me giggled as we watched this near-disaster. One or two baskets did fall outboard, but happily most of the fish landed on deck. 'I told you it was too big,' shouted Alf. 'Get the doors in, then clear the fish off the deck. We're going home.' The window slammed, and the telegraph rang even before we had everything clear of the water.

I knew Fargy was livid. It wasn't so much the lost fish – only a few baskets had gone over the side, though losing any fish is a crime to a fisherman. It was because I had ignored his warning, and because he was right and I was wrong. Fortunately, I didn't have to face him straight away. He wanted the fish cleared, so I had to go down to the fish-room first to put it away and tally up the final figure. With all the fish down, Harry and I were able to assess the total catch. It amounted to 1650 kits – not a particularly good trip by Alf Farguson's standards, but it was all first-class fish and should sell well if things went smoothly from here.

I got the lads clearing up the deck and returned to the bridge. Alf was clearly still furious. His thin, weather-beaten face was ashen, but his eyes burned brightly as I reported our final tally. He wasn't impressed.

'What do you want me to do with the trawl?' I asked.

'I want *you* to repair it. And when I say you, I mean you. The others can turn in once the deck's secured. But you can show us all how clever you are by repairing the trawl yourself.'

'OK.' I was doing my best to keep cool. I thrust into his hand a piece of paper with all the details of the trip, including the amounts taken by species, turned and left the bridge.

Steaming home at twelve knots, the wind was that bit more cutting, with choppy seas whipping sprays off the bow. The sky was grey and overcast and the air damp. And this was considered fine weather, with only the odd scudding sea coming aboard. I had a job spreading the trawl out on my own – I had to leave the winch ticking over and heave on the Gilson wire myself – but I managed it after a fashion. The net now stretched right along the fore-deck, past the winch and over the after deck. Torn, ragged holes gaped all over – a couple of hours work for all hands; for me, working without help, not even someone to fill the twine needles, it would take the rest of the day at least.

Weary though I was after thirteen days fishing, I set about the job with determination; I was always good at braiding net at speed. But after an hour stooping over, with nothing else to distract me, my shoulders began to ache. The loneliness, the empty deck and those harsh conditions made every minute drag, not to mention the embarrassment I felt when I glanced up at the bridge and saw the two deckies on watch staring down at me in comparative warmth and comfort.

I suppose when faced with this situation most men would have found an excuse to nip off deck for a drink from time to time, but I took a different tack. Determined as I was to get the job over and done with, I worked on solidly, stopping only for a half-hour meal break. By evening I'd finished the mouth and belly of the trawl and turned my attention to the open tears in the cod-end. What a shock. In the middle of this stronger double net, on the edge of the tear, was a badly chafed patch about the size of a dustbin lid, worn very thin and weak.

'We caught nothing last haul,' the decky had said when he called me out. Now I knew what had happened. There had been no fish because the cod-end had been chafed out, probably by a big stone that had eventually torn its way through. Repairing this hole was the job of our supposedly experienced bosun, and Joe had taken a short-cut. Any conscientious officer would have removed the thin, worn net; he had just stitched it back together. Whether this was for speed and to look good, or out of sheer idleness, I don't know, but he had set me up for the bag to burst upon me.

I was tense with anger when I realised that I'd taken the blame for someone else's neglect. For a moment I thought of going straight to the bridge and reporting everything to the skipper. But that wasn't the way I operated. I would tackle that later. Right now I had to remove the bad patch and insert a new piece of net. I chopped out the whole of the damaged two-foot square section, then I went down the hold to cut a piece to fit. The repair to the cod-end completed the job and I went off to report to Fargy, taking the damaged section with me.

The watch looked towards me ruefully as I dragged my weary body through the bridge door. 'Where's the skipper?' I asked. They gestured towards the chart-room behind the bridge. Then Fargy stepped out to confront me.

'The trawl's all ready, Skipper,' I reported. 'What do you want me to do with it? Lash it up along the rail or put it away?'

Fargy took a step towards me, his chin thrust forward. 'Dump it, the lot, over the side,' he snapped back malevolently

He briefly stunned me into silence. 'Righto, I'll need some help with that,' I said calmly. 'Come on you lot.' And off I went, taking the watch with me and leaving the bosun's handiwork draped over the captain's chair.

Fargy certainly was one of the old firm. I just hoped he'd look at that piece of net and work out what had happened. Maybe then he'd realise just what a waste this was. Over the next couple of days, the situation eased a little but I wanted some clearer indication that Fargy wanted me back. We were on the bridge together, as insurance rules demanded, when we steamed down the

Humber towards the dock. 'I want to sack the fish-room man,' I told him quietly.

'Why?' asked Fargy.

'Harry's a decent enough worker, but I can't have him constantly tittle-tattling to you and undermining my authority.'

I was expecting a scathing objection but Fargy's response surprised me. 'Fine, just make sure you tell him before we dock.'

Strange little fellow, Alf Farguson.

I gave Harry Petch the news as we stood together on the fo'c'sle head going alongside the jetty.

'Does *he* know?' asked Harry, nodding towards the wheelhouse.

'Yes,' I assured him, 'he does. Shows who your friends are, doesn't it?'

The next day we turned out 1666 kits on the market and my storage methods were vindicated. Our fish stood out by comparison with the competition, much brighter and fresher looking, so Harry had at least proved his worth when I wasn't down the fish-room. The sales staff were delighted. Nevertheless, they told me, I was short of my tally.

'What do you mean?' I asked. 'What did we report?'

'Seventeen hundred kits.'

'Well, the figure I gave the skipper was 1650,' I retorted. 'I'm only sixteen out and that's exceptional.' Maybe my sacking of Harry Petch was justified after all.

The trip brought in £7856 – a huge amount, and big money for me, even though the ship's expenses had to be deducted before the skipper and I took our poundage, and of course his share was greater than mine. Despite the substantial amount deducted for tax, I still picked up more than £100, half of which I banked as usual. I didn't have enough time to spend it, so I did what shopping was necessary, then checked out the Gardener's Arms before inevitably making my way to Angelica's. I decided to time it for later in the day, hoping to find her in the cosy little room where we'd spent such an exciting few hours.

All was quiet when I arrived at that big old house and climbed the bare stairway to the first floor. Music was playing faintly on her little portable radio as I reached her door. That's a relief! I thought happily. She must be in.

I knocked and heard Angie's voice approaching. The door opened abruptly and there she stood, rearing back a little in shock. 'Oh, it's you,' she said. 'I didn't expect you home so soon.'

That was perfectly obvious. Angie had retreated further than she intended, giving me a glimpse of an older man, heavily tattooed and stripped to the waist, standing close to the bed. Following my gaze, Angie glanced over her shoulder. 'Sorry, Rob. I'm a bit busy now. Can I see you later?'

What a cheek! 'I don't think so,' I replied, crestfallen. 'Goodbye.'

I turned away and moved off. I don't know why I was so surprised. What else could I possibly expect from a nymphomaniac?

CHAPTER 6
A NEW LEARNING CURVE

I spent fourteen months with Alf Farguson, taking only one trip off in that period. You needed at least one year's sea time to sit your skipper's ticket and this is what I had in mind. I learnt a great deal from Alf, an expert on the Barents Sea grounds (or White Sea to fishermen). Keeping up with his pedantic demands, and sometimes anticipating them, also helped to turn me into a decent mate. And in addition I was gaining a good name on the market for turning out quality fish.

But Alf was an old-fashioned skipper and times were changing. Some of his favourite tows lay along the old four-mile limit, close enough to take bearings from markers on the land. Towing by, I was fascinated to watch the Devil's Horn appearing on the headland west of the entrance to the Sylte Fjord, for example, helping to guide us through the pinnacles on the sea-bed. Fargy had picked out many other markers among the mountains, all of them alerting him to some hazard or other on the sea-bed close to the limit-line. I learnt them all, little realising that by the time I became a skipper these tows would once again be out of reach as the Icelanders relentlessly extended the limit.

Fargy would take his holidays for a couple of trips during the Greenland season. No way was he going to involve himself with dodging icebergs and pushing the ship through the ice-fields which pose a constant threat in that area. Sid Sparks would then take over, a skipper regarded as a pioneer of the Greenland grounds among Hull vessels. Silent Sid was a strange guy. Full of chat ashore, and even as far as the mouth of the Humber, he would say nothing from that point on unless forced to do so. I quickly learned not to ask anything about his gear or how he wanted to work. I just carried on as normal until he told me to stop, and that was a very rare occurrence.

Sid was happy with this and we got on well, even though we hardly communicated until we got back to Hull. Then it was all change. As soon as we had settled, he would drag me into town for an afternoon around the city-centre pubs. He seemed to know everyone, laughing and joking with them all. One of his favourites was the Blue Bell, and there he would make himself comfortable until his wife caught up with him and took him off to the shops.

Sid was another of the old-style skippers who had spent many an hour – fishing and steaming – standing on the bridge circumnavigating the ice-packs off the west coast of Greenland. He preferred to work the far banks, 200 to 500 miles up the west coast, and more than a week's steaming if you had to spend a lot of time detouring round the ice. I learned a lot from him about the Great Hellefiske and Little Hellefiske Banks, as well as the banks off Frederikshaab Bay, which were traditionally worked by Portuguese dory men.

Other Greenland grounds had also been discovered much nearer to the UK, in the south of the island, around Cape Farewell. Most of these grounds lay far inside the limit-lines and I was about to sail again with one of their pioneers. A number of our skippers had noticed my success in turning out the sort of top-quality fish which brought good prices at market and all were keen to have me as mate, including our top man, Rowan Berkeley. It was quite a while since I'd gone bosun with Rowan and sailing now as his mate would give me a chance to learn even more from him. But it would also introduce me to some of the most dangerous tows ever performed by Hull and Grimsby trawlers.

By now Rowan was semi-retired, spending part of the year helping out in the office and returning to sea only when the season suited him. He particularly enjoyed Greenland in late summer, when the ice-packs had broken up and he had a fair amount of open water to go at, favouring the inside areas close to land, especially at Cape Farewell. Here the current moving down the east coast tends to push the ice-fields away from the land before turning the corner and heading back up the west side of the island. A clear strip of water usually flowed around the rocks there, allowing the more daring skippers to tow close to land, at about half a mile or less, once they had managed to pick or force their way through the ice-fields beyond. Rowan liked to work a little bight in the rocks which he had helped to pioneer at a place called Avardlerssuaq. The deckies referred to this spot as the 'Caves Tow', but to Rowan it was 'Sunshine Corner'.

It was great to be back in the *St Dominic* again with our top skipper, particularly as the chief engineer was my old friend Hughie, who had first sailed with me years ago as second engineer in the *St Nectan*. Hughie was a very bright young chap, nursed by the company for these new engine rooms. He was also a fun-loving guy. Our paths had crossed a number of times over the years; we had always had a good time together and this trip proved to be no exception.

I couldn't resist slipping unnoticed into the massive engine room, hiding behind one of the three parallel diesel engines, and tapping rapidly with a spoon on the hand-rail. Hughie would rush to investigate, allowing me to slip round the back of another engine and repeat the process. With three engines to check, I could keep this up for several minutes before he found me and chased me out with a threatening cry and an oily rag to the back of the head. Hughie, of course, would reciprocate as soon as he got the chance, but that didn't happen often when we both had serious business in hand. And, for me, the business before us was very serious indeed.

Working the little bay at Avardlerssuaq meant towing very close to land, not just inside the limit-line but at times inside the baseline. These were uncharted waters and extremely dangerous. Rowan would shoot in from a mile off and close with a rocky headland pierced with caves. You could see right through them when you got near enough – hence the 'Caves Tow'. From there the tow followed the rocky shore in an inward curve at two cables or less until it approached another outcrop of rocks sweeping down into the sea to form a reef. When the last visible rock was bearing NNE it was haul quickly or come fast on the bottom. Something I hadn't so far experienced, thank God.

The tow was short but productive, each haul repaying us with roughly six big bags of prime cod. Excellent, over three hundred baskets for little more than an hour's work. No wonder Rowan persevered with it. And the tow also had another advantage – the strong current sweeping the shoreline would have us back in our starting position by the time the fish were aboard. Most of the tow was completed in around sixty-five to seventy fathoms of water, but its middle section passed across a deep hole in the sea-bed, adding to its difficulties and dangers. This was very foul ground, leaving us unable to move further off if we encountered any chunks of ice passing inside.

Apart from the size of the catch, there was only one other positive thing to say about this crazy tow; it was daylight fishing only. Thank goodness, the fish took off during the hours of darkness, making for comfortable working for the crew. The skipper could use all hands through the day and then let everyone go to bed at night. All except one, that is. And that one was me. Someone had to man the bridge while the rest of the crew slept on, and it had to be someone capable of handling the ship, keeping us in position and clear of the ice and rocks.

The short tows made it difficult to clear the fish as it came aboard, so Rowan had worked out a plan to make things easier. We took the gear in at six every evening, when everyone – apart from me – went for their thirty-minute tea-break. Then the whole deck crew would turn out to gut the fish piled up on deck while I went to tea and then to bed. By midnight, the decks would be clear and everyone turned in, the skipper included, and I took the bridge till six in the morning. It was a long, hard night, but the engineers always looked after me, often finding the time to bring me a hot drink or two.

It was eerie alone on that bridge in the darkness but I had plenty to keep me occupied. If the ship was stopped for any length of time, the strong current would sweep us down and into the land, towards the reef where a Hull trawler had been lost only a few years previously. My orders were deceptively simple: keep a mile off the islands we were working and do not get south of them. But keeping a mile off was by no means easy. Field ice constantly flowed past outside us and sometimes tried to push us towards the land, leaving me to pick my way through its outer edge. Time and again I was thankful for the searchlight fitted by the owners to the foremast. It illuminated the waters on the bow, helping me to spot the odd growler dotting the edge of the pack.

Growlers – chunks of ice that have broken away from an iceberg – are very dangerous. Composed of fresh water, rather than the salt water of pack ice, they float beneath the sea, displaying only one eighth of their true mass and sometimes bobbing in the waves below the surface. Then, if you're not careful, they pop up with a whoosh to smack a hole in a ship's bow. It was hard to pick them out among the white cat's paws of the breakers rolling towards me in the fresh breeze.

I often looked around through the bridge windows at the black night and the even blacker edge of the mountain range, so close to us. The dim light cast by the screens of the various instruments provided the only illumination, and in the absence of other ships in our vicinity my situation seemed even lonelier. The bridge was large and as I stood on its right wing – one hand on the automatic tiller, dodging the ice-floes, the other working the direct-control engine telegraph – the extent of my responsibility would often hit home. I was in sole control of the monster beneath me; everyone else, apart from the

St Andrew's Dock.

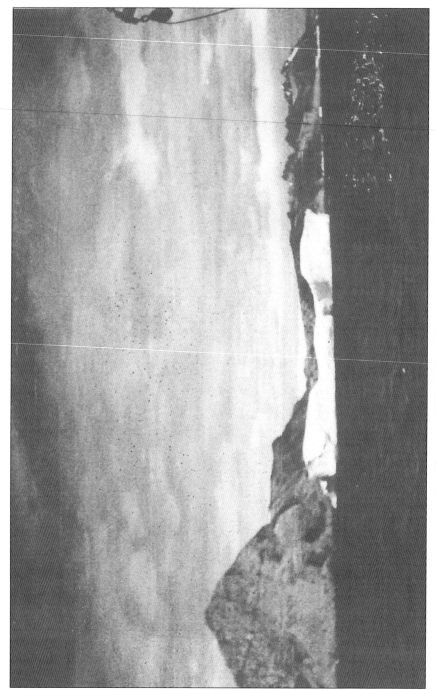

Avardlerssuaq – Distant View of Caves with Passing Iceberg.

Greenland – Cape Farewell

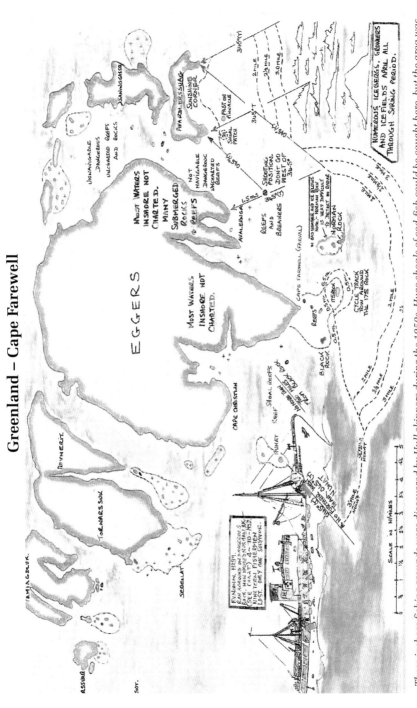

These inshore fishing grounds were discovered by Hull skippers during the 1950s. Huge shoals of cod-fish could be caught here, but the area was never surveyed completely and good charts were non-existent. Dangerous rocks and reefs abounded, and bad weather and ice were constant hazards. It was no place for the faint-hearted. The St Giles, for example, was trapped here in a massive ice-field and NW storm on Xmas Day 1972.

two engineers working hard on their auxiliaries deep in the engine room – was sound asleep. A first taste of what a skipper's job entailed, I suppose.

Come morning, I had to have the ship ready to shoot in for the first tow, in a position I had learnt from Rowan. Two of the mountain peaks differed markedly from the rest – not sharp, craggy and pointed, but nicely rounded and ideally spaced for Rowan to nickname them Marilyn Monroes. I had to line up these two peaks either side of a pinnacle of rock sticking up on the shoreline. Once the skipper arrived on the bridge, a slight adjustment and we could shoot away. We spent four good days in this precarious spot before the fishing began to dwindle and Rowan decided to move on. Would the skipper now find us a less hair-raising tow? I wondered. Certainly not!

Nor was the 'Caves Tow' quite finished with us yet. Around five-thirty we had reached the end of our last daylight tow and were just approaching the critical NNE bearing, indicating the reef, when the skipper rang the stand by bell. Aware he had no time to waste, the winchman moved quickly to pull in the warps and heave up the trawl. But disaster – a sudden buzzing noise and the electric winch stopped. Everyone on deck turned to stare at him. What was he doing wrong? Nothing to do with me, he gestured, shrugging his shoulders and turning his hands palm-up.

Now the chief came running double-quick to sort out the trouble, while on the bridge Rowan was becoming increasingly agitated, studying radar and compass as we reached the critical bearing. He had absolutely no room for manoeuvre – all he could do in these circumstances was keep on towing. The chief soon identified the problem; a trip switch had been thrown out. A quick adjustment and he had it replaced – a pretty speedy job to be fair, but just not quick enough. As the chief called up to the bridge, the after warp began to pull out. Just what we were dreading. The gear was fast on the bottom.

As we were no longer moving through the water, the skipper had to stop the engine – the risk of getting the gear tangled up was too great. Releasing the warps from the towing block aft, we transferred the purchase to the two rollers in the gallows fore and aft. Now the skipper could start manoeuvring the vessel and try to unhook the trawl from the rock or fastening down below. The warps were spread fore and aft, in our normal hauling position, except they were bar tight and wouldn't give. The strong current was pushing against the side of the ship and away from the gear on the bottom, further reducing any room for manoeuvre.

We began steadily to hove in the warps against the strain in an effort to get over the top of the fastening, but eventually something on the after end parted and the after warp began to veer aft. Still, we had made some progress; at least we'd managed to release the trawl from the bottom. Once the gear was up to the side and the after door had appeared we could identify the problem. The after cable had parted, leaving the whole of the trawl hanging on the fore end. Both trawl doors were already up. Then the fore wing appeared, with the rest of the trawl hanging down beneath the water.

Now it was down to me to get the gear in, on what we called a one-ended job. I would have to try and get a Gilson hook into a wire or strong rope down there; I'd have to do my own bit of fishing. By now it was falling dark, and the ship – unable to move with the gear floating loose over the side – was at the mercy of the current. Rowan must have been an anxious observer as we drifted ever closer to land, but he kept his nerve and didn't chase me to work faster. Fearful of panicking the crew, he only once sang out to me to remember where we were. But he certainly frightened me when I peered through the half light and made out a scattering of rocks. So absorbed had I been with my task, I hadn't noticed them before, even though they were only yards away.

Now the pressure was really on, and I struggled on in the darkness to hook up to something I could heave to the rail, glancing frequently at the murky outline of those black, saw-toothed rocks. They would certainly crunch us if we came much closer but there was little I could do to speed up the process. Finally Rowan called out once again. 'If we lowered the gear again do you think you could heave the cable aft into the towing block and clear of the propeller so I can move the ship?"

I quickly assessed the situation. 'Yes,' I replied, 'if we get the after door in first.' And that's exactly what we did, pretty sharp too, though it seemed to take ages before the winchman could lower the trawl again. Standing at the fore rail waiting to hook the messenger wire around the fore cable, I fancied I could hear the swish of waves over rocks through the darkness. The hair bristled in the nape of my neck and I was aching to get to work, but I had to wait until I had enough wire to reach aft.

Heaving the cable into the towing block took only a couple of minutes, and no sooner did I have it in place than the engines began to turn – even before I could sing out to the bridge. Rowan must have been watching the after end from the veranda. What a blessing to see our stern swinging towards the rocks as we turned away and headed out into deeper water – around twenty minutes' steaming. The boys headed off for a drink and I went up to the bridge to discuss our next move with the skipper. We still had to work out how to get the gear aboard once we were back in safer waters.

I was trying to picture a clump of net wires, bobbins and fish being dragged through the mid-waters at full speed. What on earth would that look like? It might never have been done before. On the bridge, a brand new axe was resting against the bulkhead; Rowan, it seemed, had an alternative in mind if my efforts had failed. The depth sounder showed the water shelving from the eight fathoms we'd shoaled to while we were laid. The print-out frightened me even more than the rocks and I could easily imagine the strain it had placed upon Rowan, forced to stand by and watch.

I turned to the skipper, a man looking forward to his imminent retirement. In the low light from the radar screen, his face seemed rather more drawn and its lines etched more deeply. He watched carefully as we closed with the ice-field ahead. 'I'll have to stop her now,' he said, turning towards me. 'We're coming up to the ice but we could've done to be a bit further off than this. The pressure's on you again. You'll need to get the gear in as quickly as possible. Still, you'll have a bit longer than last time.'

It didn't take us too long to get the gear aboard. Fortunately, it hadn't fouled up much while we were steaming rapidly away from the shore, although the shackles and ironware of the after wing had hooked up in the belly of the trawl. It was midnight before we finally got the gear sorted *and* we still had the fish to gut. Rowan was dodging the ship to Walkendorf Island, eight miles further north, apparently another close-in tow. I had now been up for twenty-four hours straight, and the skipper wanted to give himself and the crew the chance of a nap before daylight, so once again he sent me to bed while the bosun and crew cleared the decks. 'We'll all have to make do with just four hours,' he told me. 'We've lost so much time and I don't want to waste tomorrow's daylight.' I quickly made myself scarce.

Off Walkendorf Island stood a huge, egg-shaped rock, rising 500 feet vertically from the waves. But for a few rocks at its base it then dropped sheer to the sea-bed at sixty-five to seventy fathoms, and the side facing the sea was perfectly flat – the rock could have been sliced in two with a knife. Standing behind the winch, slacking away the warps, I looked on with some trepidation while we shot in towards this massive tower block. Even the boys squaring up the fore-deck, by now getting used to being this close to land, were looking up and giggling nervously long before we'd closed with it. They glanced up at the bridge now and again to catch a glimpse of the skipper, checking to see how comfortable he was with the situation. I was amazed at the sheer blind faith they showed in him.

'All square aft,' shouted the bosun, as soon as we'd paid out the warps and hove them into the towing block aft. This was my signal to head for the drying-room to remove my waterproofs and then carry on to the bridge. The monolith was already very close and as soon as I had the chance I took a peep at the radar. We were only cables off and still closing. Rowan was concentrating very hard, constantly moving from radar to depth sounder, then a tweak at the automatic pilot, before a glance at the compass and back to the radar. He popped a mint into his mouth, his eyes never wavering. I wondered if his mouth was dry. I know mine would have been in the same situation.

Rowan certainly took risks but they were always calculated ones. We worked the gear from the starboard side and always towed one way, keeping the port side to the shore. If we came fast on the sea-bed we would then be turning away from the rocks when we hauled. Eyes wide, I studied our situation. Rowan turned and looked at me with a grin. 'Who on earth discovered this tow?' I asked him. 'No chart has any soundings this close in.'

'Three of us actually – me, Hoggy and Leo. We dodged around this area with our fish-loupes going and worked together, even though we all came from different companies.'

We were now abreast of the flat gargantuan and only a few yards off. It was quite remarkable, I really felt I could reach out and touch it. The tow looked impossible and certainly could only be tackled in the absence of gunboats. 'This tow'll be another short one,' said Rowan, 'and the cables are liable to wear out quickly. Can you get out some shorter cables out ready for the next one?'

I left the bridge to go and organise the crew. Crossing the engine-room casing top, I met Hughie, our chief engineer, who was craning his head to scan the very top of the rock. 'I just had to come up and check it out,' he said. 'I was working on the spare engine when I looked up through the skylight and saw land. Well rock anyway. I couldn't believe it.' Then his voice took on some urgency. 'Are you sure it's safe?'

I couldn't resist a casual shrug of the shoulders. 'Ask him,' I said, jerking my head towards the bridge.

Hughie paused for a second before responding bravely. 'Well, if you're not worried, then neither am I.'

I grinned back and moved on, pondering his last remark. Why wasn't I more worried? It can only have been down to my faith in a skipper I knew so well. But for Hughie, it was faith in me. He must have thought I knew much more than I did. And why did we all trust the skipper so? I wondered. Was it because he looked so self-assured, because he always seemed to have the answer to every crisis? Attitude was clearly all important to command.

This close-in tow was another very profitable affair. However, it was only a short stretch so when I went below at tea-time Rowan still had a little time before full dark to dodge the vessel close-in for a few minutes. With our depth still at sixty fathoms, maybe he could shoot from here the next day and make the one way tow longer. I kept my usual distance off land that night and waited for Rowan to take us in early next morning. We put the gear over the side, lowered it, swung it round and started to shoot in towards the rock.

I was with the third hand in position behind the winch, slacking the wire away and streaming the warps off. Suddenly the skipper appeared at the bridge window. 'Stop the warps and screw down,' he shouted. What was going on? This was all most unusual and could have caused problems with the gear had the ship still been going full speed. But Rowan had already cut back and was swinging the ship to starboard when he told us to heave the gear back. The rest of the crew were trundling off the deck to get some breakfast before our next haul, but they soon came scuttling back when they heard the commotion.

The gear appeared and I ran to the rail to see what had fouled. Everything was fine. I looked up at the skipper. 'No problem,' he said. 'I just wanted to dodge the ship up a little.' The crew were a little frustrated by this, to borrow their expression, pratting about. Meanwhile I went to the bridge to discover what was really going on.

'What's wrong, Skipper?' I asked, entering the wheelhouse. Steering the ship by hand, Rowan gestured towards the depth recorder. The sixty-fathom bottom had suddenly shoaled right up while we were shooting away, forcing Rowan to change the range twice till it reached a six-fathom shoal. This was obviously the point at which the skipper had stopped us shooting and swung the ship away without telling us why.

'Bloody hell!' I gasped. 'I'd have had to go change my pants if I'd seen that while we were shooting. There isn't much you could have done if it was a reef. It must be a lone pinnacle. Or were you dodging a blinder?' (A blinder is rock lying just below the surface of the sea.)

'I don't know. But you're right, I nearly shit misself when I saw it.' Rowan wiped the sweat from his brow. 'This late in the trip, I think we'll just go back to the tow we know. That'll be safe enough.'

Good God! I thought. That first tow was supposed to be safe?

At the end of another fruitful day, I was on the bridge again, dodging the ship along the edge of the ice and thinking about the scare we'd had. Six fathoms was close; the ship drew three when fully loaded. Still, we could only have another couple of days left. I dropped the side window and swung the bridge-top searchlight to starboard as the icy-cold night air cut in. I swept the area; the field ice was getting thicker. We would have to circumnavigate it or push through it when we left. I felt weary all of a sudden. Maybe it's time I stopped for my skipper's ticket, I thought. If the gaffers will let me.

We were hauling later in the day, when one of the more mature members of the crew spoke up. 'I've seen Mother Carey's chickens,' he said, voicing an old superstition which held that if the seagulls sitting on the water begin to dip their heads en masse in order to swill their backs, it's going to blow within twenty-four hours. Standing behind the winch, waiting for the doors to come up, I studied the seagulls carefully. They were settling on the water awaiting the bag of fish they knew would soon appear. Sure enough, many of them were ducking their heads beneath the water. Much of this weather lore often came true and I didn't fancy trying to get through that ice if a gale started up.

Next time I was in the wheelhouse I mentioned this to the skipper. 'I've not seen them,' he replied. 'But the sparks says there's a depression coming in from the west so I'm planning to move soon anyway.'

'If those mollies are anything to go by, it'll be here by dark tomorrow.'

'Mmmm,' Rowan was thinking hard. 'We'll have to go soon. But it's daylight fishing here and I don't want to lose a full day.'

'Couldn't we do some damage if we tried it in the dark? You couldn't pick out the leads with the searchlight. You have to have some daylight.'

'Some daylight, yes. We'll catch the morning's fishing, set off at dinner-time tomorrow and be home for Tuesday's market. That'll do nicely.'

Sure, I thought, as long as we can get clear of the ice by tomorrow night.

The next day we shot early in the morning, managing three short tows by eleven-ish. Rewarding tows too, the best as usual being the dawning haul. But by now I was getting fairly anxious. Would Rowan actually leave as promised or would he try to carry on? Happily, he resisted temptation; we took the gear on board and started steaming south. The skipper was running inside the pack ice, hoping to see some breaks where the current changed direction at Cape Farewell.

It was late afternoon and the boys had cleared most of the deck before we spotted a gap. It was only a narrow lead, but it appeared to run as far as we could see, and we hoped it would continue right through the approximately three-mile wide strip of ice. The wind whipping over the starboard rail from the south was showing signs of strengthening. The halyards and the wires in the rigging began to sing, but the ice-covered sea remained unmoved.

Reducing our speed considerably, we weaved our way along the winding gap in the ice. Eventually it petered out, leaving us to push our way gently through the loose ice-floes. In the fading light, the fish was clear and the boys busy securing the deck. On the radar, the edge of the ice was gradually approaching and as it began to thin out the sea was getting rougher. Soon we had nothing but the odd ice-floe and growler before us, still very difficult to spot in the dark among the mounting seas, the growlers disappearing in the swell before shooting to the surface at the last minute. The bosun and two look-outs joined me in working the searchlight and watching from every point of the bridge until we were well clear. Then it was full speed for home in the stiffening gale. Thank goodness Rowan had not left it any later.

On our homeward voyage I suffered a little accident which was to bring me mixed fortunes. Only forty-eight hours from home, the weather had moderated and we were tidying up the deck as we approached the Outer Hebrides. I was at the hatch-top, keeping the net and floats off the coming as the Gilson man lowered the trawl into the net hold. Suddenly he lost control of the winch and the trawl dropped six feet, trapping my hand between the metal floats and the coming. After describing him in a way I'm sure he would never have heard before, I discovered I'd broken a knuckle. That would certainly ensure I wouldn't be back for the next trip. It was time instead to stop ashore and sit for my skipper's ticket.

CHAPTER 7

MIXING WITH THE UPPER? CLASS

The plaster on my hand wasn't conducive to paperwork. Thankfully though, it was no bar to studying and observing as I had a number of smaller qualifications to pass before I could even start on the skipper's certificate. Our first-aid lectures taught us rather more than simple first aid, including extra on anatomy and how to use the contents of our medicine chest. Helped only by the *Ship Captain's Medical Guide*, once in charge of a trawler we would be expected to act as our own ship's doctor.

I was already certified as a Radar Observer but now I was expected to take the next step up and complete the Radar Simulator course. I was also told to do a marine fire-fighting course with the local fire brigade at some time during my stay ashore. But my main schooling would take place at Hull Nautical College. Here budding skippers and mates were taught separately from the rest of the pupils by an ex-master mariner called Harvey. The curriculum was extensive – taking in everything from ship construction and collision regulations to celestial navigation by the stars – and would take two months or more to absorb.

We were a class of about a dozen. Two were resitting their mate's ticket and another three brushing up on the weak points of their skipper's certificate, having failed at the first attempt. Anyone who failed a paper could be re-examined if they returned within a month. Of course, I knew at least half of the class, some of them since we had all been decky learners together. Among them was my old pal Eddie Woolford, who laughed when we met up again because we'd also studied for our mate's ticket together. I couldn't resist taking a dig at him. 'So, smart move, Eddie! You've decided to use my brain to get you through this one as well.'

'You what!' he replied. 'More like you expecting me to do most of the research.'

'I suppose we do make a decent team when the chips are down,' I conceded.

'Too right. And I suppose you'll be expecting me to fix you up with a date as well.'

'Don't you worry about that. I'll sort myself out. If we get any spare time, that is.'

Our lessons took place in two or three classrooms in a prefabricated block in one corner of the grounds, separate from the main school building so the schoolboys didn't bother us even though we operated during the same hours. The first couple of lunchtimes most of us set off together to Hessle Road for a sandwich, but we ended up instead in the local pub with a pie and a couple of pints of beer. This didn't suit me at all. I always felt sluggish afterwards, and it was no help with my studies. Mr Harvey wasn't very happy either. 'Carry on like that and you're much more likely to fail,' he warned us starkly.

I was driving into town, so I was able to go a little further afield at lunchtime and eat on my own at a working man's café run by a friend of my father. I had updated my car since my bosun days and now had a good second-hand Ford Consul in a nice, jazzy pale turquoise. The front bench seat and the radio with a speaker in the roof above the windscreen were unusual for those days, and I thought they seemed more with it.

One afternoon one of the boys, by name of Danny, arrived back late for class. He had been to the main building on some financial matter and was now spluttering and salivating about a female he'd spotted over there. 'Have you seen the headmaster's secretary?' he said, as we settled ourselves down. No, was the answer. We had all submitted our papers through Mr Harvey and his colleague. 'Wow! She's stacked. You should see the size of her bristols. They're massive. I couldn't take my eyes off 'em.'

None of this surprised me – indiscreet and prone to exaggeration that was our Danny. But that very afternoon his description was proved correct when Jane – for that was she – entered our domain for the first time. Jane was a pretty provocative name to fishermen since most of them spent hours in their bunks reading about her nude namesake in the *Daily Mirror* comic strip. When the head's secretary entered the classroom, clip-clipping her way to Mr Harvey's desk, everyone in the room appeared to freeze. Like her comic-strip counterpart, Jane's curling blonde hair fell to the shoulder. Her silk blouse was open at the neck, the buttons down the front seemingly under considerable strain. Her bust must have been at least a thirty-nine inch Double D. A tight black skirt wrapped around a very slim waist further emphasised her tiny bottom. Could it really be strong enough to support all the weight above?

A very low wolf-whistle came from the back of the room, eliciting a glare from our teacher. Jane approached him, holding out some papers. 'Mr Harvey, you didn't sign last month's figures. Could you do it for me now, please?' Back she stepped, doing her best to cover her obvious charms with the rest of the folders she was clutching. Working in a boys' school, I'm sure Jane was used to being ogled, but these were men. She tried not to look us in the eye, paying close attention to the pictures on the wall behind the tutor's desk. I was sitting on the front row, at the desk furthest away from her, studying a manual, my elbow on the desk, head resting on my hand. I probably appeared the least interested of us all, though in reality my eyes never left her.

Spotting me on the fringe of her line of vision, she flashed me a brief smile, then gave me a second glance when I raised my eyebrows in response. I smiled again, but Mr Harvey had shuffled the papers together by now and was handing them back to her. Our last sighting of Miss Sexy was of two nicely rounded buttocks jumping alternately against the tight black skirt as she clipped her way out the door.

Mr Harvey quickly brought the class to order. Time to focus on the blackboard and ship stability, with talk of centres of gravity, metacentric heights and righting levers. But come the end of the day all the talk was of Jane. Eddie sounded off first. 'Did you see young Dasher trying to give that secretary the eye? As if she'd be interested in the likes of us. She's older than us anyway.'

That was probably true, but only by two or three years. She looked about twenty-seven or twenty-eight, but my bet was that she was still unattached.

In fact, Mr Harvey had intimated as much. 'I don't see why she wouldn't go out with one of us if she was approached the right way,' I said.

'So you think you could persuade her, Don Juan?' scoffed Eddie.

'Maybe, if I've a mind to.' The rest of the gang jeered. 'We'll see.' We all laughed and set off home.

If I was going to make good on my boast I'd have to do it quickly while Jane still remembered me. A day later I dowsed myself in splash-on and applied a good aftershave before I left for college. 'Smells like a whore's garret in here,' groaned one of my pals when I arrived. But Harvey thrust us into our work before anything else could be said.

The final period of the day was usually devoted to individual study, brushing up on areas of weakness – usually signals or the thirty-two ship's articles which had to be learnt word for word. Instead I went up to Harvey. 'Do you think the library will have a book on the stars and constellations?' I asked. I would have been been amazed if he answered no. This was the Nautical School, after all.

'Probably,' he replied.

'Could I borrow it now, do you think?'

'I suppose so, yes. Go along to the main building and ask Miss Webb to show you where the library is.'

Ah, so that was Jane's surname. I left the room unnoticed. The others were all too busy concentrating on their work.

I found Jane behind her desk outside the headmaster's office. She was wearing the same tight skirt, but today with a Scandinavian-style blouse. It was patterned and elasticated beneath the bust, making her breasts stand out as if on a platform. I was careful not to even look at it while her eyes were on me.

She looked up as I approached. 'Hi,' I said with a grin. 'I'm looking to borrow a book and Mr Harvey said you'd show me where to find the library.'

Returning my smile, Jane pointed towards an open door. 'Just off the main hall, first door on the right.'

'OK,' I hesitated. 'How big is it, 'cos I'm not sure where to start? I don't know how the books are arranged. I'm looking for a book on stars. Could you direct me to the right area?'

Pushing back her swivel-chair, Jane stood up and set off for the library. She was quite tall for a girl, coming above my shoulder in height. A good sign, I reckoned. Tall girls are always on the look-out for tall men. As we walked along, I tried to keep on her shoulder so she wouldn't think I was ogling her from behind. Once in the library, Jane headed straight to the shelves, running her fingers along the spines of the books. I seized my chance to move in close and peer over her shoulder. She didn't mind at first, but I was too adventurous, allowing my cheek to get too close to hers. Suddenly she veered off, giving me a sideways look.

'Sorry, Jane. Was I crowding you? I didn't realise. It is Jane, isn't it?'

She nodded and smirked knowingly.

'Hi, I'm Rob,' I continued, offering my hand.

She grasped it briefly. 'I think you'll find what you want round here.'

'I think I already have,' I parried back, a gleam in my eye.

'I'll leave you to it then.' She turned to go. 'I think you'll manage from here.'

'It was really kind of you to help me,' I concluded. 'I hope I can do something for you some time.'

Eventually I found a book that looked useful but I still needed a reason to seek Jane out again. 'This is just what I need, thanks,' I said, back at her desk. 'I'll use it tomorrow but how late can I return it?'

'I like to get away from here by four-thirty if possible so you'd need to get it back by then.'

I thought I'd better double-check. 'OK, so if I leave it too tight you'll be gone by four-thirty?'

'Certainly not much later. I like to catch the bus on Anlaby Road before five. They get pretty full after that.'

'Right. Well, that's fine then. Thanks.'

Back in the classroom, my mates viewed me with suspicion. 'Where have you been for the last half hour?' asked Eddie.

'The library,' I replied in all innocence.

'Which library?'

'The school library in the main building, of course.'

Eddie narrowed his eyes accusingly. 'Have you been sniffing around?'

'What on earth do you mean?'

My mock indignation fooled no one. 'Whey hey!' cried my pals. Then Harvey, unaware of our conversation, brought us to order.

At four o'clock the next day, when the rest of the class gathered up their books and pads, I stayed behind, copying out stars from the major constellations. I wanted to use up half an hour before I returned the book. The school grounds were empty by the time I went across to the main building on the dot of four-thirty, but there was no one around when I got to Jane's desk. I wandered in and out of the main hall and the library, but still no sign. Surely she couldn't have left early? No, her handbag was still beneath the desk. I moved away a little and waited. After a while the headmaster's door opened and out came Jane, looking pretty vexed. I approached her apologetically as she glanced at her watch. 'Hi! Here's the book I borrowed. I didn't know whether to put it straight back or not.'

'I suppose it's better that I've seen you return it,' said Jane testily, packing things away into the top drawer of her desk and locking it. 'I haven't time to put it back now, though. The headmaster's made me late for my bus. They'll all be packed by the time I get to the top of the street.'

'If you're going out Anlaby way, I could give you a lift in my car. I'm going in that direction. I live in Swanland.'

'You've got a car?' It wasn't the first time I had heard this. No wonder Jane was surprised. Few people ran a car at that time, but I could easily afford one on my mate's wages.

'Yes, I need a car living out there. The buses only run every hour and a quarter. It's right on the street outside. Do you want a lift?'

Jane picked up her handbag. 'Why not,' she said. 'Thanks very much.'

Jane was pleased to see that my car wasn't some old banger, and she liked the colour too. I settled her on the bench seat beside me. 'I live in Anlaby

Common,' she said. 'Perhaps you can drop me at the end of my street.' Off we went, chatting as we went along. I took the opportunity to show off the radio with the speaker in the roof, and Jane was impressed that I was sitting for my Captain's Certificate, as she called it. She was much more relaxed than before and we laughed a lot. She was fun, singing along when the speaker started blasting out a country and western number.

'Do you like country and western?' I asked her.

'Oh yes, I'm quite a fan.'

'Well, there's a group playing at the Rising Sun. Tex Rimmer and His Cowpokes or something. Would you like to come for an hour or so? It's not far from where you live.'

Canting her head to one side, Jane looked askance at me for a moment. But all she saw was an open face and an expression of innocent enquiry.

'I could pick you up at the end of your street, if you like. Then I won't drink too much.'

'OK,' agreed my buxom passenger, giving me the strong impression that she was starting to size me up.

I dropped Jane off as agreed and we arranged to meet in the same spot at seven-thirty. Then, with a cheery wave and a song in my heart, off I went. A couple of hours later I was back at the top of the street with only a few moments to wait before Jane appeared and climbed in the car. She was wearing a pale-blue dress with a square neckline and buttons up the front, partly covered by a little jacket nipped in at the waist.

A few minutes later we arrived at the Rising Sun, a large, country-style pub on the edge of an estate. We were a bit too late to get a good table and had to settle instead for one set back from the little stage, and off to one side. But when Jane removed her coat I was quite relieved we weren't at the front. The low, square-cut neckline of her dress exposed a balcony of lascivious titillation which – much to my annoyance – immediately caught the eye of all the males around. While waiting for our drinks I spotted a fellow across the room grinning at me and nodding. Who on earth's that? I wondered. Then I realised he was one of the guys resitting his mate's ticket. We budding skippers didn't mix with them much, but I was pleased to see him and acknowledged him in return. Now the gang would get to know that I was out with Miss Webb, and I wouldn't have to say a thing. One in the eye for Eddie, then.

The lively country and western group played with a good swing which soon had us tapping our feet and enjoying the happy atmosphere. The only problem was they weren't on long enough. Not much over an hour really, just enough time for me to down a couple of beers and a dram, while Jane, to my surprise, had a couple of Bacardis. It was a bit of a let-down when the band left early for another gig, leaving us with piped music and a game of crown and anchor.

After some small talk and another drink or two, I mentioned to Jane that a country and western programme would soon be starting on the radio. 'We could listen to that if you want. I know a spot with a particularly nice view of the river on a clear night like this. We could drive down there. I'll even treat you to a meal if you like. I'll get a couple of bags of crisps and we could listen to some more country.'

'Wow! Entertainment and a meal thrown in,' laughed Jane. 'How could I refuse?'

Armed with the crisps and a couple of small bottles of Britvic orange bought at the bar, I drove us on to Welton and then up to Welton Heights. Fortunately, I hadn't drunk too much. I'd still have been able to walk in a straight line if I'd been stopped. Up on the high road, I backed into the open gateway of a field, then switched off all the lights and settled down to listen to the radio and snuggle up to Jane. The moon reflecting off the tide rips of the Humber was a magical sight, silver jewels lighting up the river as it flowed towards the junction of the Trent and the Ouse.

Already mellow from the two Bacardis, Jane loosened up even more as she listened to Jo Stafford singing 'Blanket on the Ground'. She was obviously quite prepared for a bit of kissing and petting, and pretty soon I was massaging her neck and shoulder. I'd already pushed her coat off because she was warm, so it was no problem slipping the shoulder of her dress down her arm – strangely the top buttons were already undone. Our kisses heated up with our gyrations and I let my hand sweep gently down her chest to scoop out a floe of firm pink blancmange topped with a cherry. I was quite overwhelmed by the firmness of a breast so large, caressing it and covering it with little kisses before extracting the other and nuzzling into them both.

Jane was arching her back, apparently reaching the heights of ecstasy as I continued to experiment with my licks and nibbles. But I still wasn't moving fast enough for this siren of sex. Breathing heavily, she suddenly pushed me away, lifted her dress up at the back, deftly slipped her panties over buttocks, thigh and knees, and kicked them to the floor. Now, without warning, she turned and pushed me down across the front seat of the car until the back of my head was thrust against the door. Hungrily she unfastened my trousers and pulled them down my thighs, my underpants soon following – a simple enough procedure since my feet were still resting on the floor. Giving me no time to adjust my position, she then took me in hand and mounted me, while from the speaker above Frankie Lane belted out 'Rawhide', the beat seeming to add momentum to her lust. *'Riding-riding-riding'*, chanted Frankie, as Jane crouched down like a jockey, keeping pace with the rhythm.

I would have enjoyed myself more had it not been for Jane's pendulous breasts, now swinging so much that they kept smacking me in the face, making me splutter and gasp for breath. My God! Miss Webb wouldn't entertain the likes of us eh, Eddie? How wrong could you be? She was a man-eater!

I said nothing to the gang about Jane's passionate performance, although I did intimate that we'd got on rather well for a first date, leaving them to draw their own conclusions. Jane continued to show an interest in me, but we were studying harder and harder as Harvey flung ever more subjects our way, and spare time was at a premium. Jane appeared to have other escorts anyway, so the odd time we got together it quickly developed into a heavy petting session. The trouble was that, given her inclination to enhance her already exceptional sexual charms, she soon drew attention, and I had to be careful in choosing where we went. I wouldn't have felt comfortable escorting her in company with Mum and Dad or their friends, so opportunities were rare.

We took our exams one at a time, helping and encouraging each other as the weeks went by. Any exam you failed had to be retaken before you could carry on, and eventually about half the class, including Eddie and I, had got through the lot, leaving us with only the oral to face. That, however, was the scariest of all. The reason – a certain Captain Logan, the most fearsome of examiners. As an ex-Merchant Navy man, he seemed to despise fishermen, prizing nothing more than the chance to show up their incompetence, and responding to any wrong answer with a torrent of abuse. His presence had turned many an accomplished applicant into a gibbering wreck. One bright student couldn't function at all in front of him. After several fruitless attempts he tried to take his oral in Grimsby. But Logan got wind of the plan and moved the exam back to Hull. Imagine the horror on this young man's face when he discovered the change, just two days before his date with destiny. Still, it remains a bit of a puzzle when you consider what frightening scenarios he must have faced at sea.

Eddie and I were booked to go in front of Logan on the same day – along with dopey Danny, not a man noted for thinking before he spoke. My half-hour exam was scheduled for ten-thirty and I was distressed to hear that Eddie would follow me at eleven. It looked like Danny would precede me, not exactly the guy I would have chosen to warm Logan up. The examination room and Logan's office were both on the top floor of the Burton's building on the corner of Whitefriargate. It had no working lift, so you had plenty of stairs ahead of you to reach the fourth floor.

I arrived fifteen minutes early to allow myself time to catch my breath and compose myself. The partition dividing the offices from the passageway was polished wood below and glass above, giving me a view through the open door of the outer office straight into the examination room. What I saw there made my stomach lurch. Captain Logan's bellicose face was blood red, expletive following expletive as he reprimanded a shell-shocked Danny. Staring with dismay at the man I was supposed to convince of my competence as a trawler skipper in little more than ten minutes time, I felt a nudge on my arm. Unable to contain himself, Eddie had arrived more than half an hour early, hoping no doubt for some moral support.

'Is that him?' he whispered. I nodded, my eyes riveted to the scene before me. 'Bloody hell! What has Danny said to him?'

'I don't know,' I mumbled. 'I just hope I don't come up with the same thing.'

We watched as Danny uttered something that succeeded only in whipping Logan up into an even greater frenzy. The examiner's great bulk loomed over our pal as he ranted at Danny's stupidity, following it up with some very inventive swearing. Danny was bent backwards like a bow in his efforts to escape the full blast of Logan's wrath. Meanwhile the examiner's middle-aged secretary sat in the outer office and carried on typing, quite unconcerned. She could have been listening to Housewives' Choice.

Logan's belligerent attitude had still come as something of a shock. Perhaps he was trying to test our reactions under duress. 'I think I'll pack it in now,' moaned Eddie. 'I always wanted to be a bus driver anyhow.'

Though feeling no better myself, I did my best to reassure him. 'Come on,

Ed. Plenty of others have passed before us. It's just a matter of thinking before you reply. Don't blurt things out like Danny.'

Before we could say anything more, the interview was over and Danny was scrambling his way out the door like a man trying to escape a snapping dog. He stared at us white faced and saucer eyed, but the secretary called me in before I could quiz him any further. No more time to think then as she led me before Logan, who had now returned to his desk. 'Please confirm your name, date of birth and the certificate you're testing for,' he said, eyes fixed on the piece of paper in his hand.

The examiner's face remained straight, unemotional – indeed almost bored – as he continued to question me, mainly regarding the thirty-two ship's articles. I had been expecting this and had learnt them all off by heart, but he probed further to make sure that I'd fully understood them. After going on to ship handling, he next told me to remove a sextant from its box and find the error on it. Mr Harvey had warned us about this. Logan would look carefully at how we retrieved the instrument and how well we handled it.

Following the examiner's instructions, I took the sextant to the window and, with no sun available, wrote down the readings using chimneys and roof-tops for a sight. To my horror, I discovered an error way above the norm. Panicking a little, I returned to the window and quickly tried a different set of objects. I was worried that Logan would run out of patience but still I arrived at the same ridiculous figure. 'Well?' said Logan, prompting me for the figure I'd calculated, excessive though it seemed. I've blown it, I thought. But Logan seemed happy enough. It must have been another ploy thought up by the wily old captain to give us an extra test.

The examiner softened his attitude a little after that. Soon the exam was over and he handed me a piece of paper to give to his secretary on my way out. On it was the one magic word, 'Passed.' I left her to type up the necessary papers, sucked in several deep breaths and returned to Eddie in the passageway. I couldn't do much to brief him before he too was called in, but at least he'd been spared any ranting. The secretary told me I'd receive my Board of Trade certificate in the post. Now all I had to do was go through it all again for my insurance certificate.

I was in a daze, completely euphoric. Nevertheless I paused long enough to see how my pal was getting on. Logan was peppering him with questions, but Eddie, though very pale, at least seemed to be avoiding confrontation. I looked out of the fourth-floor windows at Princes Dock opposite, where two more new trawlers were fitting out before joining the deep-sea fleet. It would be good to be back, but I wasn't quite finished with exams just yet. With that other certificate still to pass, I scampered down quickly from these classrooms in the sky.

CHAPTER 8
MY EDUCATION CONTINUES

The exams for the skipper's insurance certificate were no easier than those for the Board of Trade, but we seemed to get through them quicker. The point is that I passed: now I was fully qualified to take a fishing vessel anywhere in the world as long as it was for the purpose of fishing. A bit scary when you thought about it. All I had to do now was to persuade an owner to give me a command. Passing my certificates may have proved me capable of navigating and handling a ship, but it didn't demonstrate my ability to catch fish. Only my past skippers could testify to that.

With my reputation for turning out high-quality fish, I was expecting to find a berth as mate pretty easily and a ship soon became available. It was one of the older ones – a bit of a disappointment after my recent experience of the bigger vessels – and its skipper, college-educated Timothy Edgar, only three or four years my senior, had little more experience than me. A skipper for little more than twelve months, he had done all right to start with but couldn't yet be considered a real success because his last few trips had been poor. Tim was small and fresh faced – baby-faced to the deckies – and his high-pitched voice had earned him the nickname of 'The Squeaker'.

I was surprised at the owner's decision. I was expecting a place with a more experienced skipper, not a man who knew little more than me. But Timmy was glad that I was signing on with him. He wanted a mate of some stature and when I saw the crew who had latched themselves on to him I could see why. A pretty laid-back individual, Timmy had unwittingly managed to assemble most of the company's hard cases and layabouts. It looked like being a tough trip for me. We were in the St Amant, a decent enough ship, although not a new one. Like my first ship, the St Apollo, the Amant had a single bridge. She also had a good fo'c'sle forward – important in keeping the crew happy – a fine turn of speed, better in fact than some of the newer vessels, and a good fish-room.

My problems began soon after we sailed. On our second morning at sea I had the three a.m. to breakfast watch. Instead of going below after breakfast, I decided to sort out the day's work and headed for the forehold where we kept the trawl spares. There I found the working party was under strength, consisting only of the bosun and the daymen, including the two decky learners and the fish-room man. One of the watch-keepers was missing. I also discovered that the trawl spares comprised just one complete trawl, fixed and ready. Common practice was to have smaller sections of the trawl ready prepared for a quick replacement job if only part of the trawl was damaged.

'Where's your other watch-mate?' I asked the bosun. Of course, one of them would be steering the ship, but what had happened to his pal?

'He's cleaning the bridge. This old man likes the bridge cleaned up each morning while we're steaming.'

'So do most skippers. It doesn't need a fully fledged deck-hand, though.

Send one of these decky learners up and let's have your mate down here. We don't need two lads to fill needles and fetch and carry.'

'But that's the way we've always done it on the *Amant*.' The bosun looked uncomfortable, shrugging his shoulders restlessly. 'I don't think *they* like change.'

'I don't suppose they do. It's nice and comfy for them,' I sneered, steadying myself against the plunge of the bow over the steady swell. 'But by the look of it we're not getting enough work done down here. We need a lot more parts preparing. If they're ready to use we can save time when we get fishing.'

As mate, I was a share-man like the skipper, paid purely on results. Neither of us could afford to lose time on the fish. 'Tell all watches that a decky learner will be cleaning the bridge in future. The deck-hand will be working on deck.'

I set to organising as much work as possible for the rest of the day – no easy task as the crew were used to sorting out so much themselves. I would have to introduce changes steadily and subtly with this mob. They soon started chuntering and muttering whenever I altered something. I didn't want to turn them against me from the start, but I would clearly need to push them, hard cases or not.

The Squeaker decided to take us to Bear Island to catch a trip. He had been pretty lucky in finding fish there in the past. But he wasn't quite so fortunate with the weather on this occasion.

The Bear Island grounds present no difficulties for a skipper as far as the sea-bed is concerned, with few of the hills and deep gullies typical of most other grounds. Apart from a sheer drop into deep water on the western edge of the Bear Island shelf, about sixty miles offshore, the ground is fairly flat, shoaling steadily right up to the island itself. But the weather in these latitudes, almost 500 miles inside the Arctic Circle, is a different matter. You nearly always face ice and snow in the winter; and in the summer, cold, damp fog.

And on this particular trip the wind never eased up either. A Force Five or Six was constantly puffing up from the north and west during our first week's fishing, coming off the ice of Greenland and Spitzbergen (Svalbard), as a series of lows passed through. Although it seldom blew hard enough to stop us fishing, it was sufficient to keep the seas slopping over the bulwarks. Still, the Squeaker kept the fish coming aboard, with a couple of bags of fish each haul. They were only codling though and unlikely to fetch a good price.

To be fair to him, our skipper tried a few different tows around the bank. There were few other ships around to work with and wherever he went it was the same story – small fish every time. The trip was dragging by. Small fish take longer to process and move off deck, and the endless measly weather wasn't helping either. Eventually Timothy decided to try the deeper water off the edge of the bank, where the bigger fish can usually be found. Working at depths of 220 to 230 fathoms, we needed to put out a lot more wire – about 650 fathoms' worth – which the old *St Amant* found much harder to drag around, particularly in such scuffly weather.

We certainly caught the bigger fish we were looking for, but in smaller quantities. So now the skipper faced a bit of a dilemma. Stay with the smaller catches of better quality fish while dragging three-quarters of a mile of wire around, or return to the shoaler water? As it happened, the decision would soon be made for him.

Turning the ship round to double back on our tow was made twice as difficult by the rough seas endlessly rolling towards us. As the ship came round, it was bouncing over a ten- to twelve-foot swell, extending almost at right angles the wire warps pulling the trawl. In all side-trawlers, these warps pass through a rolling block at the stern known as a towing block. Under the extra strain here, the fore warp suddenly slipped into a sharp niche in our new-style, built-in towing block and parted at the block.

Oh calamity! Yet again I was facing a one-ended job, getting the gear in on one wire. These were always tricky, especially when as now you were bringing the trawl in to the narrow after deck, with only the after derrick at your disposal, instead of the more spacious fore-deck, where you could also use the various wires from the mainmast. This particular job was made even more dangerous by the bad weather and the position of the break. A towing wire would normally part on the bottom, fairly close to the trawl gear. When it parts nearer the block, the wire drops down to the sea-bed, doubling the amount you're dragging behind you.

Following normal procedure, we knocked the after warp out of the block and steadily hove it up, bringing the after door to the after gallows. Here the after men managed to unclip the door fairly quickly, still dodging large dollops of water. Anchored as it was by the after gallows and the huge length of fore warp dragging along the bottom, the ship had lost some of its buoyancy and we were taking on more water than usual.

This, of course, was my baby. Only I could determine what would happen next. When the seas weren't knocking me back, I had to be right on the job at the ship's rail, watching every fathom of wire as we hove it in, making sure none of it was stranded and liable to part. The skipper was on the bridge, windows closed and nose pressed to the glass, well protected from the swirling fog and the cold, salt spume. It looked like it would all be down to me. There was little he could offer in the way of advice anyway.

When the after end of the actual trawl arrived clear of the water at the gallows roller, only the first two bobbins of the ground rope were visible. My job was to get the after Gilson lifting wire hooked onto the rope beneath these bobbins so we could heave them up to the derrick top. The grey waves slopping over the bulwark rail were giving me just a few brief moments of respite when the water receded enough to expose more bobbins eight feet below the rail, allowing me to swing the hook into position. Time and again I failed to connect as tonnes of water poured aboard, scattering or knocking down anyone bold enough to come to my assistance. But I was going to need some help. Only by leaning right down over the rail could I get close enough to do the job, and I needed someone to grab hold of my legs and trap them against the bulwarks with the bulwark wire. My knees would then be resting on the rail, allowing me to hang down much further outboard. However, every time a sea washed over us, both my helper and I would be submerged until it cleared through the scuppers.

I asked for a volunteer and much to my surprise my call was answered by one of the earlier skivers from the bosun's watch. I was glad enough, though.

He was a big, strong man and I was confident he wouldn't let go of me, no matter how much water we were under. My life support knew just what was required. Grabbing my thigh-booted legs under his arms, he hitched me to the rail so I was hanging half over it, then locked us in position by grabbing the bulwark wire. Even now, the seas submerged us both two or three times when the ship rolled before I managed to connect.

Only once, after I'd taken a breath and gone under again, did I feel the grip on my legs briefly slacken. This quicker sea had apparently caught my pal full in the face, temporarily choking him with salt water, but he never let go. With the wire now in place, I had to work out how to tell the winchmen to heave before I lost the connection. As I rose out of the sea, I was coughing and spluttering too much to shout. I waved my arm but the winchmen couldn't see me. Luckily one of the lads sheltering on the boat deck had spotted me and relayed the order to the winch.

Once the winch had taken the weight on the wire, it was time for me to get back inboard. I had to wiggle my legs quite a bit though before my pal realised what was happening and hauled me in. I found the bobbins and net hove up high to the block. It was a lot of weight for the after derrick, especially as we were still dragging the rest of the gear along the bottom – fore door and fore warp included. Our situation was also aggravated by the constant westerly wind and sea, which were gradually pushing us into the shoaler water on the bank, so ensuring that more wire would reach the bottom. I had to get another wire on those dangling bobbins – and quickly.

When the next incoming sea had subsided enough I once again stepped to the rail. Armed with another hooked wire, I reached out to secure a hold on the giant's necklace of twenty-inch iron beads now towering above me, right up to the derrick top. As I did so, the ironware suspended over my head seemed to drop by a foot. I turned and glared at the wire man at the winch. Was he losing control? But no, that wasn't the problem. I haven't lost anything, he quickly signed back to me. Now I glanced up at the derrick block where the hook was still tight up. Fucking hell! The problem must be the Samson post supporting the derrick. Its base plate was sagging into the steel boat deck so the post itself must be leaning over. I'd have to take some weight off it immediately.

Another sea poured aboard, but once again I stepped right into it to fix this second hook. Then I signed to the winch to take the weight before the ship lurched again and put the derrick under even more strain. I soon got the job done, but I still got a shock when I saw how much weight had been suspended above me. It was a miracle the wire hadn't parted. We struggled on, gradually working the incoming gear along the deck until it was possible to bring the forward wires into play. Many hours later, the gear and warp were all inboard and we were effecting repairs. But by that time I'd been up for thirty hours straight.

We continued to fish in this miserable weather for another few days until our time was up; then we scrambled the gear aboard, secured it along the rail and set off full speed for home. We would have to repair and refurbish the gear, but I was confident we could do that once the weather improved. And there was nothing we could do steaming full speed in these conditions. But the weather never picked up. It remained poor until the day before we docked and it looked like we'd be arriving in the Humber with the deck in a shambles – no derricks topped, fish-washer stowed, trawl removed or even decks cleaned. This was unheard of, and I would be to blame.

Early on our penultimate morning I was on watch. The forecast was good for the coming day and the weather was obviously improving at last. Now was our chance. We could do it all in one go, but it would probably take all day to finish things. When the bosun relieved me at three a.m., I issued my instructions. 'If the weather stays fine, call all hands for breakfast.'

The second deck officer took a step back, studied my face and then moved up close. 'This skipper never works all hands,' he told me confidentially.

'Maybe not,' I replied in similar tones. 'But the situation demands it and I'll answer to the skipper. Just do it.' I knew it would be around nine o'clock before the skipper turned out of his bunk, and by then we'd have got nearly two hours work in.

Four hours later, the shout of 'All Hands' called me for breakfast, along with the rest of the crew. It wakes you up with a shock when you're expecting to sleep on so I knew there'd be plenty of snarling. After breakfast I chased the crew out the mess and led the way on to the deck. We started by chopping down the trawl from the rail to overhaul it and make any repairs – not a long job after a trip to Bear Island where the sea-bed causes little damage. We finished the trawl within a couple of hours, quicker than I expected, and were soon lashing it up ready to put down the hold. That was a good start but we still had plenty to do.

Now I split the crew, taking three men with me to unshackle the bobbins and start replacing the bobbin wires, while the rest steadily put the trawl down the hatch forr'ard. The men down below had passed some replacement bobbin wires to those of us amidships, but it looked as though we'd need some new bobbins too. 'Stop putting the trawl down and hove us up a couple of twenty-inchers,' I shouted, and the mumblings and grumblings began again.

The lads carried on with the job, making snide remarks about my calling all hands. 'We're just being messed around,' they whined. Their complaints gathered in volume until it became obvious I was meant to hear.

I decided to bring this to a head. Flinging my crock spanner down on the deck, I strode purposefully forward to confront the small crowd gathered round the hatch. 'What's with all this moaning and groaning,' I asked them. 'Anyone would think you were suffering. What's the gripe?'

They were momentarily nonplussed. 'It's that cunt,' said the ringleader, nodding his head towards the bridge. 'Why call out all hands.'

I glanced up at the bridge front, where the top of the skipper's head was just visible through the open window. So that was it. This crowd was miffed because The Squeaker hadn't questioned the all hands call.

'Listen,' I said, 'it wasn't the old man who called all hands, as well you know. It was me. We've only got today left to clear the whole deck and stow everything away.'

'It didn't need all hands,' this sea lawyer insisted. 'We could have got the lot done in half a day.'

'I very much doubt it,' I replied. 'Even with all hands we won't get finished as quickly as that. Let's just get on with it and we'll see what happens.'

I turned and retraced my steps to the waist of the ship. After that things became electric. Using the Gilson wire, my little gang and I continued reeving the heavy bobbins on to the new wires. Meanwhile all around us men were quickly touting other lifting wires around the deck to get things clear. Even when sent for a drink, the boys were barely off the deck for ten minutes before they were back of their own accord. They were obviously trying to prove a point. It suited me; we'd get the job done quicker.

But in all the rushing around, a bobbin balanced on a wing bollard above my hand was dislodged just as I was pushing a becket into place. Down came the bobbin, briefly crushing my hand. It didn't fall far, but I felt the crack of bone and my hand soon swelled up like a balloon. No one took much notice and I carried on as best I could. The job was soon finished and by now it was dinner-time. The standing watch went off to eat as normal, but the rest of the deck crew had a surprise up their sleeves. 'Can we stay on deck until second sitting?' they asked.

I knew what they were up to. They wanted to prove that they could get most of the work done before the afternoon session. Our next task – stowing the derricks – needed supervision. The bosun had gone to dinner with his watch, so I opted to remain and see the job done. The lads tackled it with exactly the same gusto as before. Men scampered up the rigging to release the derrick from its working position, and then on up to the cross-trees to chain it up, before rushing aft to secure the after derrick. I'd never seen such enthusiasm.

We were still on the job when the first sitting came back on deck. But still the lads carried on for another ten minutes to finish it off. 'There you are,' said one. 'We knew it wouldn't take all day to clear the deck. Why call all hands then?'

I didn't bother to point out that it was only by using all hands that we'd got through so much work, quite apart from the extra effort they'd all put in – apparently something of a failing with them in the past. And we hadn't quite finished yet, though a single watch could easily handle the remaining work. Nevertheless I decided to give them best. 'Well now, who'd have thought it?' I said with a grin. 'You've proved me wrong, so we can restart the watches. You can all go and turn in now. Leave the rest to the bosun's watch for the afternoon. Off you go.'

I'm sure one or two of them had their suspicions. Why did I seem so happy to be proved wrong? In addition to their unhappiness with the skipper, they were beginning to feel they'd been conned.

As for the skipper, he was secretly delighted that I'd used all hands and got through the work so quickly. 'I suppose the men were pretty annoyed,' he said later on, when I was on watch. 'They don't like working all hands on this ship, you see.'

'That's true of any ship,' I cut in. 'They'll just have to put up with it.'

'Yesss, but they could get awkward.'

'You're in a much better position to get awkward than they are. Anyway, it's all done now.'

Arriving in the Humber, we were told to land our catch in Grimsby. It appeared they wanted codlings and our trip was expected to bring a better price there than in Hull. I'd been in ships that landed in Grimsby before, but that was only as a decky, when I could go home overnight while the ship was discharging. This would be my first time as mate, and I'd have to be up throughout the night to keep an eye on proceedings. Most of the deckies, including some of the awkward squad, headed for home. However, the agent stirred things up by giving the skipper some cash to dish out to anyone wanting a sub, so several of the crew stayed on, mostly engineers and cooking staff.

The *Amant* moored up to the fish quay as night approached, the hatches were loosened, and I could at last relax for a while. Having dealt with customs and the agent, the skipper invited me into his berth for a couple of whiskys and a beer or two, and I was pleased to accept. I'd still have chance for a little lie down before the lumpers started unloading in the early hours. Both weary after such a demanding trip, the drink had more effect on us than normal and we were soon scrambling into our bunks.

I was woken three hours later by the noise of the fish stages being rigged from quay to hatches, ready to discharge the catch. Tumbling out of my bunk and slipping on my clumpers, I headed aft to the galley to get a coffee before going on the quay. Judging by the noise emanating from the big dining cabin below – which also served as sleeping-quarters for some of the after squad – the lads were back on board after a boozy night ashore. They were making quite a racket, singing and shouting, but I made no attempt to get involved. I wasn't feeling that bright myself.

There was plenty of activity on the fish market. Up to fifty men were working frantically to unload our ship before the sales. I soon identified the foreman lumper and made myself known to him. He greeted me doubtfully but he seemed a decent enough chap so I just wandered around for a while. I did find a couple of things to disturb me. For example, they put an extra cod on top of the weights when they weighed out the eight-stone boxes. This, I was reliably informed, was to counteract the weight of the boxes themselves. And any fish that fell out of the boxes as they were dragged off the ship and along the quay tended to be kicked into the dock rather than picked up. I put the lumpers right about that, but I could see that my constant surveillance was beginning to irritate them.

They tried to get rid of me by pointing out the noise coming from the after end of the ship, where the cabin was obviously the scene of a hectic dispute. It sounded like the racket that issues from the Ghost Train at Hull Fair. With every crash or shout, the men working on the dock or the ship turned and stared at me, obviously expecting me to quell the uprising. Eventually an extra loud bellow and the sound of breaking glass embarrassed me enough to go and investigate. I marched swiftly down the quay, leaned out, grabbed the edge of the boat deck and deftly swung myself on to the after deck, then made my way into the companion-way and on down the steps into the cabin below. How on earth could so few men be making such a din? Just four of them were squabbling in the middle of the room, while the bosun – very much the worse for drink – was about to launch another empty bottle in the direction of the scuffling quartet.

I stepped forward smartly and removed the bottle from the bosun's unsteady hand. Eyes glazed, he shot me a disdainful look, mumbling something along the lines of 'fucking, interfering busybody', all the while trying to remove the cap from his one remaining bottle of beer. I grabbed this too and threw it into the top bunk behind him, bringing forth a stream of abuse as he struggled to climb on to the bench seat and retrieve it. As he reached across the bunk, I applied my shoulder to his buttocks, heaved him over the bunk-board to the middle of the cot, and left him kicking and squirming like a beetle on its back.

Now I turned my attention to the source of most of the noise, the quartet around the central stove. The thick metal mizzen mast came down through the cabin alongside the fireplace, and the cook and two deckies looked to have the skinny little fireman backed up against it. I was a bit surprised to see the cook behaving so aggressively. He always seemed a calm, level-headed individual and it was very unlike him to be involved in a three-against-one situation.

I stepped between the warring parties, thrusting the threesome back from the fireman. 'Hey, what's the matter with you all,' I shouted, 'attacking one man.'

'He started it,' they tried to protest. Then the fired-up little stoker took a swing at one of them over my shoulder.

I pushed him back against the metal pillar. 'Whoa!' I snapped. 'Give me a chance. I'm trying to help you here.' And with that he smacked me in the mouth. Shocked at this unprovoked attack, I reacted automatically. I walloped him on the jaw and his head jolted back on to the metal mast behind him.

'That's just what we were trying to tell you,' the cook pleaded. 'He started it, throwing punches at everyone.'

Once again, this aggressive little man lunged at me, arms flailing. I pushed him back again and he started kicking out at my legs and private parts. I let fly with more venom this time, throwing a much harder punch, but as I did so some delayed reaction suddenly took the fireman to the floor. I missed him entirely and instead hit the metal mast behind him. Now, whether through tiredness or my earlier drinks with the skipper, I had completely forgotten about my injury and had used my damaged hand. When my fist hit metal, the cracked bone splintered and came right through the back of the hand. It left me hopping around for a minute, the damaged member tucked underneath my arm.

Meanwhile the cause of all the fracas was laid gasping by the stove. 'I can't breathe,' he said. 'My rib's broken.' When the drunken little trouble-maker had collapsed, he had fallen across the foot-high brass rim of the ash-pit, catching himself right across the ribs.

With my hand oozing blood, it was down to the other three to pick up the unfortunate and carry him to his bunk. He carried on protesting vigorously, insisting that he wanted to see the skipper. Things seemed to calm down a little after that so I left in search of something to wrap around the wound. A decent-sized handkerchief did the trick and then it was back to the fish market. I continued to check up on the lumpers, while they in turn viewed my bloodied hanky with suspicion.

A short time later the skipper called me from the bridge veranda. 'Can you come up here, Bob? We've got a problem.' I jumped back aboard and made my way to the bridge. 'We're in here,' called The Squeaker from the chart-room, where I found both skipper and sparks standing over our erstwhile kick-boxer, now laid out moaning on the settee. 'He claims you pushed him down on the cabin stove and broke his ribs.'

I looked down with disdain at the weasel-faced little engineer. 'I didn't push him. He collapsed of his own accord. Mainly through too much drink.' I didn't bother adding that if I had landed my punch he would have finished up on the deck anyway. 'From my observations he hasn't done any serious damage.'

'How the fuck do you know?' snapped the perverse little trouble-maker. 'You haven't examined me.'

'The trouble is, he's insisting on going to hospital,' muttered The Squeaker, pulling me to one side.

'I don't think there's anything wrong with him,' I whispered. 'Give me a minute. I'll soon find out.'

But the skipper ignored me. 'I can't afford to deny him treatment if he's injured,' he said, asking the sparks to get in touch with the port radio and request an ambulance. It was still only five in the morning.

Meanwhile I pretended to make my peace with the obnoxious fireman, kneeling down beside him to offer my apologies. 'I'm sorry you've been injured,' I said, 'but it was an accident.' Then I feigned a problem with his ear. 'Can you turn your head towards me while I take a look? I continued. I leaned over to examine his perfectly good ear, deliberately resting my hand on his supposedly injured side, and quietly but steadily pressed harder and harder for a full minute or so. Eventually the sustained pressure made it difficult for him to breath and he thrust me off, complaining all the while. But he'd have reacted much more strongly if he really had a broken rib.

I immediately reported my findings to the skipper, now restlessly pacing the wireless room awaiting confirmation that the ambulance was on its way. Yet I still couldn't persuade The Squeaker to accept there was nothing wrong with my adversary. 'He wouldn't be complaining like this if he wasn't in pain,' he insisted. Eventually the ambulance pulled up on the fish quay and, with some difficulty, we manhandled the casualty on to a stretcher and off the ship. The skipper accompanied the patient to hospital to make sure he didn't make any outrageous claims, while I stayed behind to monitor the final landing figures.

At the sight of this prone figure and my damaged hand, the lumpers quickly put two and two together. I was obviously some kind of thug who ruled with a rod of iron. Their foreman approached me. 'Why haven't you gone to hospital as well?' he asked. 'That hand looks bad. You need to get it seen to.'

'I can't. I've got to remain on the market until all the fish is landed.'

'There's a first-aid post at the end of the quay. It's open all night. I'd go there and get it dressed properly if I were you. It'll only take you twenty minutes or so.' That seemed to make sense, so off I toddled.

Two nurses were on duty when I reached the post. 'How did you do that?' asked one, when she uncovered my hand.

'I slipped down the ladder and smacked it against the bulkhead,' I replied, deciding it was better to lie.

'It looks like you've got a splinter stuck in the back of your hand.' And taking hold of a large pair of tweezers, she started tugging at the piece of bone protruding through the skin.

Eventually though, my protestations persuaded her to relent. 'Can't you just leave it alone and strap it up?'

'OK,' she replied, 'providing you promise to get it treated properly when you get home.'

Grateful for a proper, well-padded dressing, I returned to my position on the fish market just in time to see our skipper return in a taxi, a blanket hanging over one arm. His baby face was twisted into a snarl as he booted the backside of our supposed casualty back to the ship. I was amazed. I'd never seen The Squeaker as angry as this before.

'What happened, Skipper? I asked, as the fireman passed me.

'I've never been so embarrassed in my life,' our captain snapped. 'A well-spoken foreign gentleman examined that creep over there. "There's nothing wrong with him", he said. "He's just drunk." Then prat-face there kicked off. "You're a four-eyed scrob," he said. "You don't have a clue what you're talking about." All I could do was apologise and drag him out of there. And I resent having to pay for a taxi to bring him back.'

Then for the first time the skipper noticed the big dressing on my hand. 'What on earth have you done there?' he asked. There was no point lying so I told him the truth. 'It's just a pity you didn't connect,' he replied. 'It might have saved us all some trouble. You can get it sorted in time for the next trip when we get back to Hull.'

Reluctant to explain the full extent of the damage, I just left it at that.

CHAPTER 9
AT LAST PART OF FISHING'S ELITE?

The Squeaker was devastated when it became obvious my broken hand would prevent me from making another trip. He even suggested I might go back without using it, just to run the job. That would be impossible on a trawler, of course. Anyone else would know that – but not Timothy Edgar.

To be honest it didn't bother me too much. The Skippers' and Mates' Annual Dinner and Dance was due in a week or so, and it would be my first opportunity to attend since joining the Trawler Officers' Guild. But our firm was less happy about my enforced spell at home and booked me on a Radar Simulator Course. I still needed to get my hand sorted out as well. A pot would make writing too difficult, so I went to consult Ginger, the medic who assisted the doctor at the fish dock surgery, and he agreed to apply a splint and strapping to give me more flexibility.

The simulator unit had been set up in the main building of the Nautical School. Four cubicles were each equipped with a radar set, while an adjoining room contained a control unit capable of simulating any sea-going scenario. The idea was to set up a scenario with several vessels approaching or crossing. We then had to plot them, determine their course and speed, and take evasive action with the controls attached to our radar screens.

Only eight places were available on the course, two per cubicle, and six of these were reserved for Merchant Navy captains. Just two therefore were open for trawler skippers, and I was given one of them. Was that significant in any way? I don't know. But the other slot was taken by Skipper Tom Tucker, a man who had recently joined us from another company and was certainly reckoned a bit of an up-and-comer.

Of course radar plotting was right up my alley. Tom was very happy for me to guide him and in partnership with him I had little difficulty in passing all the early tests. We were streets ahead of any of the Merchant Navy captains, who all became very chummy as the week-long course progressed. Even though Tom and I hadn't met before, I knew him by reputation and we got on very well. Short and stocky, Tom shared my sense of humour and had got up to some outlandish tricks in the past, among them poaching right under the noses of the Icelanders, and attempting to ram their little gunboat.

I found the course very enjoyable and useful, making some good friends and extending my knowledge of radar plotting, while out of school hours I was able to meet up with my old friends when they each came home from sea. We were all looking forward to the Skippers' and Mates', to be held in the so-called Jackson's Ballrooms above the Jackson's Bakery shop in Paragon Street – a move up-market from the previous venue, Beverley Road Baths. It was an evening dress do really, though a number of the mates in particular, myself included, didn't have evening suits. And even those who were properly attired didn't always cut the debonair figure envisaged by the organisers – due mainly, I fear, to the amount of alcohol consumed beforehand. One or two had abandoned all attempts at elegance and were wearing broad, brass-buckled leather belts to hold up their trousers.

I went to the dance with two or three pals: Terry and his brother Kenny, plus Geoff, our shore-based friend. Terry and Geoff had each invited their current girlfriends. Terry's date was a little cutie called Audrey Standish. We'd first met her roller-skating many years ago and they'd just met up again. Geoff's girl was smart and well-groomed, but, it would be fair to say, not exactly besotted with him. On our arrival we also met up with my college buddy Eddie. Eddie had booked for the dinner and the dance, but the rest of us all had cheaper tickets for the dance only.

We three single men were rubbing our hands in anticipation, looking forward to meeting up with some bonny girls. I felt sure that Skipper Ashburn would be there, and I was hoping to latch on to the vivacious Janine. Harry Gold and his Pieces of Eight, a popular local band, had just struck up when we arrived. Downstairs they were still eating so there were just a few small groups of lads and lasses around, mostly shore-based people attached to the fishing industry. We got our drinks and stood back to observe the arrivals from the dining-room below. Among the first to appear were Eddie and his family, including two nice girls he later claimed were his cousins. They settled down close to the dance-floor and Eddie came across for a natter, keen to discuss some of the pretty girls he'd seen over dinner.

My head was swinging round every time a new group entered the ballroom, and Eddie at last took pity on me. Skipper Ashburn and his party, including his luscious daughter Janine, *were* in attendance. Apparently every young buck around Janine was keeping an attentive eye on her too.

'Don't forget you've a couple of attractive cousins with you,' I reminded him. 'You need to pay them some attention before you go looking elsewhere.'

'Don't worry,' he reassured me. 'I don't think I'll have any chance to compete.'

All this had got me thinking. I'd have to be smart off the mark if I was to grab Janine's attention before the vultures started circling. Best be bold, I decided. Go up to her as soon as she arrives. Positioning myself with a view of the top of the stairwell, I waited for my chance and was soon rewarded. Skipper Ashburn and his wife were just appearing at the top of the stairs, while Janine trailed slightly behind chatting to a friend in another group.

I set off to intercept her on the pretext of returning my empty glass to the bar. Brushing past some other guests, I nearly bumped right into her. 'I'm sorry,' I said. 'Oh hello, it's Janine. How lovely to see you again, and lucky as well. Perhaps you could give me the benefit of your expertise on the dance floor again. We didn't get much of a chance at the last one, did we?'

Janine gave me a lovely smile and introduced me to her friend.

'Look, we're not far from the bar,' I continued. 'Perhaps you'd let me buy you both a drink while you think my offer over.'

Thoughts of the bar getting busier seemed to do the trick and I was in. We stood near the bar talking for a while. 'Mum's trying to persuade Dad to retire,' said Janine.

'There's not much chance of that,' I replied. 'Not while he's still one of the top skippers.'

You don't just walk away from a position you've reached purely through your own skill and experience. Besides the gaffers would do everything they could to hang on to him.

We had nearly finished our drinks and Janine's friend excused herself so we could take the floor for a foxtrot. My partner was an accomplished dancer so I had to do my best to impress if I wanted to keep her coming back. For her part, Janine seemed happy and gay enough. Not only was she pretty, she also managed to give me the feeling that she thought I was wonderful, looking up into my face with an admiring twinkle in her eyes. With my arm around the slim waist of such a buxom but shapely girl, I was loving every minute. But we had to call a halt after a couple of dances. 'I'd better go join my parents for a drink,' said Janine. 'I haven't spoken to them since we came in.'

My mates had commandeered a small table at one end of the room, so I got myself a drink and went over to join them. A number of ribald remarks followed: apparently I'd almost rugby-tackled Janine as she entered the room; nor it seemed did I know the whereabouts of her waist, my hand falling way below the mark while we were dancing. I ignored it all and sat rather smug as I watched Janine turning down one or two hopefuls who approached her for a dance. It was hardly surprising. Like me, she'd only just sat down. I intended to give her the chance to rest for a while and time it just right before I asked her again. The boys had twice replenished my drink so I had some catching up to do, but everyone was drinking plenty.

Pretty soon two of the boys got up to dance with their girlfriends and it was time to make my move. But when I finally stood up, Janine was busy talking to another woman, so I paused for a moment before I moved forward. Suddenly a tall, slim figure hove into view. It was none other than Sandra Johnston, clad in a close-fitting, blue-satin evening dress. Advancing purposefully round the edge of the dance-floor, she was obviously looking for a partner. But, lovely as she was, I was in no mood for her prudish attitude.

I turned quickly to return to Janine, only to find myself confronted by another female acquaintance from my past. Face beaming and eyes sparkling, blonde hair flicked out in gay abandon, Christina Larsen searched my face for a reaction. Wrapping her arms around my waist, she thrust her pelvis into mine and leaned back to admire me.

'Christina!' I gasped. 'Where on earth have you sprung from?'

Christina and I had enjoyed what sophisticated types would call a little affair some time back, but I remember it better as a red-hot, lustful association. She was always keen to make things permanent, but we had lost touch when I was taken ill and she went away to study.

'Leeds, actually,' she quipped.

The lower half of her body still thrust forward, she was swinging from side to side with the music. The two lads still at the table were watching this with some amusement and I was beginning to feel a little embarrassed. Certain others might be watching, after all. 'Come on,' I said, taking her arm. 'We might as well have a dance while you explain.'

We moved on to the floor and Christina slipped easily into my arms as we swung into another dance. 'So, you're over from Leeds then? What are you doing there, still studying?'

'No, I'm at the hospital – St James'. I'm working there as a radiologist.'

'So you're just visiting your mum and dad, are you?'

'Yes, well Mum actually. Dad's away at the moment.'

'Wow, that's bad judgment. It's not like him to miss anything like this. He usually works it so he's home.'

Christina's father was a skipper with a well-deserved reputation as a tyrant. He certainly gave me a rough time when I sailed with him.

'I think he had an engine problem and had to go into Norway,' she explained.

In common with our previous liaison, Christina was dancing very close, her pubis hard up against my thigh, sharing what she thought would interest me. Glancing round, I saw Janine had been snapped up by a smart-looking lad. But I didn't care about that at the moment. Christina was exciting company.

We danced together a few times and she chose to remind me of some of our raunchiest moments. 'We were pretty young at the time,' I reminded her. 'I assume you've a bit more decorum now.'

'Oh yes,' she assured me. 'I've a lot more of everything now, enthusiasm included, especially for a big guy like you.'

We stopped a couple of times for a drink. Christina knocked back two large glasses of white wine, making her moves even more romantic as she snuggled her head into the nape of my neck when the lights were dimmed during the slow dances. But she had some depressing news as well. Apparently her mother was in town at another function and would be picking her up in the car at the end of the dance.

After a while I excused myself to go to the toilet, which was just outside on the landing. Chris took the opportunity to go too and we walked out together. Needing to freshen up a little, I had a quick rinse and groomed my hair while I was in there. Back outside, Chris was alone on the landing, leaning against a door marked 'Private'. Quickly she waved me over, pushing back on the spring door as I approached, and dragged me into a darkened room, illuminated only by light reflected through a window from the street below.

'The bulb must have blown,' she whispered. 'I've tried the switch.'

We seemed to be in a store room of some kind. I could just make out spare chairs and tables stacked to one side of the room. 'I spotted this place when I came out of the toilet,' Chris continued. 'Just the thing for a bit of privacy. Now we can really recall old times.'

Without hesitation, my little nymphet moved in and clamped her lips to mine. Her luscious, silky mouth and the passion she displayed were a gratifying boost to the ego. Although we could barely hear the music from the dance, Christina continued to sway and rub herself against me as we clasped each other tightly. Once again her yielding body, scent and subtle feminine movements quickly had me aroused and gasping. Some females giggling outside sent us moving away from the door and towards the tables, with Chris still clinging on to me.

I pushed her up against one of the oblong tables and we continued to gyrate our hips. A V-cut piece in the middle of her square-necked dress revealed her cleavage and – given our previous familiarity – I decided to plunge right in. Sliding my hand into that inviting neck-line, I began to caress her breast, all the time sensing her breathing faster and faster. Not to be outdone, Christina clamped her hands to my buttocks, spreading her legs and pulling me into her. 'Oh Bob, I want you,' she moaned.

By now I was almost panting with desire. Switching my hands to the bottom of her dress, I hitched it up to her waist. Underneath were what felt like silky lace panties. Excellent, no elastic round the legs! Chris helped me extricate all that I had from my underpants. Then bending her backwards on the edge of the table and pulling the crotch of her panties to one side, I slowly but firmly entered the tight moistness within. So turgid was my swollen cock-end that I could feel every internal muscle and fold my delightful young lover had to offer. With the pulsing of my blood heightening all my senses, I continued thrusting into her, ever more aware of Christina's smooth cheek against mine and her gasps of breath in my ear.

When she wrapped one of her legs around mine, drawing me in even tighter, I knew she was just as enthralled as me. Our muscles tensed whenever voices approached outside, making these magical moments even more exciting. Then we reached a mutual climax and our breathing stilled. 'Oooh, wonderful.' Christina sobbed. Then she sighed. 'That was wonderful.'

We clung together while she nestled her head in my shoulder and I nibbled at her ear. Then voices outside and a bump on the door from some silly girls going to the ladies brought proceedings to an abrupt end. We tidied ourselves up and exchanged a couple of pecks of gratitude before peeping out the door, making sure all was clear and moving quickly out across the landing. Just as I was checking my fly, the door to the Ladies opened and I spotted Sandra out of the corner of my eye, but I pretended I hadn't see her and hurried on.

Back in the ballroom, Chris and I merged and joined the crowd halfway through a quickstep. Then we worked our way around the floor, slowly taking stock of where everyone was. Sandra had returned to the room and stared meaningfully towards me before moving towards a group of friends, while the gang had managed to hold on to our small table. 'Shall I introduce you?' I asked Christina. The boys were chuffed to see such a pretty girl at the table and most amused to discover that her father was the hard-faced Lugs Larsen.

Christina charmed my friends, even having a couple of dances with two of the boys. Eventually she pointed out that time was pushing on, but she insisted on one final dance before she had to leave. 'Mum'll be waiting outside,' she explained while we were on the floor. 'She'll want to make sure I get home early enough. I'm on duty in Leeds in the morning.'

I escorted my love partner down one floor to the cloakroom. Before she went, she pushed a piece of paper into my hand. On it was a telephone number written in lipstick. 'This is the number in the nurses' home,' she said. 'If you ring, someone will bring me to the phone. Now don't come any further. Mum'll be waiting and I'll have to dash to the car. I hope you'll be in touch soon, though. Bye.'

She sprang down the last flight of stairs in her usual lively way, hair bouncing as the light caught her blonde highlights. Then she was gone without turning back. Sadness gripped me in the pit of my stomach and I stifled a

A Christmas to Forget – the Ice-bound St Giles off Cape Farewell.

St Andrew's Dock.

little sob as I stared at the empty doorway. Then I turned and ran back up the stairs.

With the gang still settled at our table, I picked up on the chatter and finished the drink waiting for me there. Then they all jumped up for the next dance. It was a slow waltz so they all felt confident. Meanwhile I decided to go to the bar and replenish my drink. It was still fairly busy and I had to wait to place my order. 'Well now,' came a voice in my ear, 'and when do I get a dance? You've been happy enough to ask me in the past.'

The slinkily dressed Sandra was right by my shoulder. 'Hi, Sandra!' I greeted her. 'Of course I'd spotted you. I was going to ask as soon as I'd quenched my thirst with a nice gin and tonic. I don't suppose you'd be interested. You're not into alcohol, are you?'

'Oh, I can be,' she countered, eyes flashing. 'If the time is right.'

What on earth did she mean by that? What was it about this place that made women radgy?

'Would you like one too?'

'Yes, please,' she replied. I bought our two drinks and we stood sipping them at the side of the floor. 'What a shame we've just missed the slow waltz,' she continued. 'I seem to remember you were pretty good at that.'

'What do you mean?' I said indignantly. 'I'm pretty good at the foxtrot and the quickstep now too.'

'Well, there's a foxtrot just starting. Let's catch it quick.'

Without further ado, I supped my drink in one and placed the glass on a nearby table. And much to my surprise, so too did Sandra. Out on the floor, I put my arm around her. Her silky dress made me feel as if I was touching her bare body – something of a distraction, I must admit. Noticing that we weren't going so smoothly, Sandra decided to blame herself. 'I'm sorry, I seem to be a bit out of time,' she giggled. 'It must be the couple of drinks I've had.'

'Oh, so you'd already had a drink before I bought you one, had you?'

She grinned at me, glassy eyed. 'Yes, that's why you'll have to take me home later when the dance finishes.'

'Oh right,' I said. Nothing like setting out the programme for the night. I was a bit apprehensive about going back to that big house outside town. After all, it wasn't me that got her tipsy, was it?

The gang had clearly spotted my new partner, but I never got the opportunity to introduce her. She insisted on clinging very close to me for the rest of the night, smiling at me through sleepy eyes and occasionally resting her head on my shoulder. Still, she knew what was what. 'We'd do best not to wait for the last dance,' she announced. 'It'll make it difficult for us to find a taxi.'

I agreed it was time to go but I hung on for a while when they started to play a cha cha. I liked 'Tea for Two', both the words and the tune. Under the circumstances, however, neither of us were nimble enough to follow the beat, so we soon left the floor and went down to collect Sandra's coat.

The taxi driver seemed to know the house. It was set back in extensive grounds and Sandra stopped him half way down the long drive. 'Everyone will be in bed and I don't want to wake them,' she said. 'I hope you'll come in for a coffee, though. Come on, we'll go round the back."

I turned to the taxi driver and paid him off reluctantly. I didn't want to stay too long in this big house. The driver was well aware of my predicament. 'I'll hang around for half an hour or so for an extra ten shillings,' he offered. 'I'll have missed all the dances turning out by now.'

'Thanks,' I said. 'I'd appreciate that.'

Sandra had a key to the kitchen-door and I followed her round the back of the house, noticing on the way a big bay window overlooking the sumptuous gardens.

'Best just make it a quick coffee,' I said. 'I've told the taxi man to wait.'

'There was no need to do that,' she said sharply. 'I could easily have ordered you another when the time was right.'

'It's OK,' I replied. 'He's prepared to hang around for a bit.'

The back door opened through a small porch into the breakfast area of a very large divided kitchen, with a carpeted dining section and a small two-seater couch in the bay window. On the far side of the window, a door stood ajar. 'The back stairs are through there,' said Sandra. 'They lead up to the first floor. That's where the main bedrooms are.'

Good Lord, stairs front and back. Not many houses around like this, I thought.

Sandra wanted to take me through to the lounge, but I was wary of waking anyone and elected to have my coffee on the little couch instead. Still, she went through into that part of the house anyway, throwing her little bolero coat over the back of a chair and soon returning minus her silver-strapped dance shoes, a glass of sherry in each hand. She handed a glass to me. Not exactly coffee, and sherry wasn't ideal for bringing my hostess down from the clouds. It was probably the first thing she'd seen in her dad's drinks cabinet.

Sitting down close to me, she put her free hand around my back and rested her head on my shoulder. 'Let's drink a toast to our friendship,' she said, raising her glass. 'I hope it'll only grow stronger.' We both sipped our drinks and she pulled me towards her, kissing me on the cheek. 'I had hoped our relationship might be a bit closer by now,' she continued. 'I can be just as loving as the others, you know.'

Putting her glass aside, she began to massage my chest and stomach and kiss me smoochily on the lips. Then, without warning, she slid her hand down the front of my trousers, right into the rocket silo, and grabbed the weapon readying itself to meet her. With my sherry in one hand, and the other pinned behind her back, I was completely defenceless, and Sandra was already at work on my trousers. I tried to put my drink on the floor and squirm away but, intent on her goal, Sandra followed my every move. We both finished up rolling on the floor. I had my pants around my knees, while my new-born sex siren had her satin gown hitched up to her waist, revealing that she'd already removed her panties.

The sight of those naked thighs and all they led up to was enough to extend my love-making equipment to the full. Grabbing my buttocks, Sandra spread her legs. I drew up a little while she slid down and together we brought about the automatic docking of my rigid member into a very juicy haven.

My God, was Sandra hot inside. Our connection lit me up like a neon bulb. The transformation of this demure young coquette into a ravenous sexual predator excited me so much that I entered into satisfying her with great gusto. As I gathered momentum, my love partner began to gasp and moan. But I had to bring her back down to earth – and quickly – when she started to shriek. 'Careful there, you might wake your family.'

'It's all right,' she panted. 'Grandpa's the only one who sleeps at the back of the house. And if he gets up it'll only be to go to the toilet.'

Only Grandpa! Only the founder and head of their family business! I was pretty sure I knew what he would say if he discovered what his grand-daughter was up to through that slightly open door at the foot of the stairs. The door was only six inches away from my feet. Perhaps I might improve the situation by pushing it shut with my toe. Easier said than done, though. By extending my leg downwards I disengaged my love tackle, causing Sandra to grasp my buttocks once more and ram me home to full penetration. Despite my distraction, and much to my amazement, everything worked perfectly, except that my climax was somewhat delayed. Sandra must have had a ball until I eventually achieved my goal.

Looking down at Sandra's perspiring face, hair damp and sticking to her temples as she lay catching her breath, I marvelled at the reproductive animal that until aroused lies buried, sometimes deeply, within us all. I eased my weight off her, kissing her in gratitude all over the face and lips. Then we both stood up, trying to restore a little decorum to our appearance in the coolness that follows after sex. I was surprised how short a time had passed since we entered the house, and Sandra was still intent on making me the coffee she had promised.

From her flushed cheeks and the slightly embarrassed look in her eyes, Sandra was struggling with mixed emotions as she kissed me demurely but fully on the lips when we said our goodbyes. What's got into these women? I wondered, returning to the taxi. What makes me such an attraction? Then the answer came to me in a rush. I was a successful, *single* mate on the verge of going skipper, that's what was unusual. It had been a hectic night. Time for me to go back to sea.

CHAPTER 10

SKIPPER JEKYLL OR MR HYDE

My hand still wasn't quite right – it now had a hump on the back – but my grip had returned and I was fit enough to work. The company sent for me to sign on as soon as they heard the news. But their choice of ship was rather unexpected: I hadn't sailed in the *St Alcuin* since I was a decky learner. And the skipper was another surprise. It turned out to be my new friend, Tommy Tucker. Tom wouldn't have asked for me, I was pretty sure of that. So what lay behind the move?

It was common knowledge that the company had commissioned a new ship, taking its business for the first time to a major shipyard up in Scotland. Tom was flavour of the month – bringing home big catches while simultaneously sticking it up the Icelanders, who were once again trying to extend their limits – and he was considered a shoo-in for the new vessel. So I was hoping they'd put me in the *Alcuin* ready to take over as skipper when Tom moved on in a couple of months time.

I also knew that Tom hadn't spent any time in Greenland with his former company, and the gaffers were keen for him to get some experience in that area. I'd made that trip many times as mate so it made sense to put us together and send us off for the Greenland season. Tommy was amused when he learned I was going to be his mate. At least he knew what a help I'd be with the radar plotting once we got among those Greenland fog-banks.

For once we were lucky and the Atlantic was flat calm as we set off across the Great Divide. Some days we even had the sun on our backs and it gave me chance to get everything ready in good time. Little Tom was very chirpy at the way things were going and full of chat about his current reading, a spy novel by Ian Fleming. On my evening watches he would offer me a dram of rum, asking if I wanted it shaken, not stirred. The crew too were in a jolly mood. They were particularly taken with 'Sixteen Tons' and 'Big Bad John', two new songs then filling the airwaves with stories about coal-miners and their courage, something fishermen felt a great affinity with. In short, it was a pretty happy ship that made its way towards the ice-ridden waters of that most difficult of fishing grounds.

To my delight Tom decided to ignore the Cape Farewell grounds. The ice-fields were thinner than normal so we could pick our way through without having to sweep maybe an extra hundred miles around the outside. We also passed by the Kitsissut Islands, another bad fishing ground, known to fishermen as the Kitsiguts. Eventually we decided to shoot on Semersok Bank, in the middle of Julianehaab Bay. It had plenty of potential and was probably the easiest ground in the area.

Here, inside the main ice-fields, there were no ships and not much in the way of loose ice, just the odd growler and the occasional iceberg – hardly unusual for Greenland at this time of year. Tom decided to shoot on the south edge of the bank and tow in towards the land. On most grounds, a seventy-fathom shoal was the best bottom. If you went any deeper than eighty or ninety fathoms, you were in trouble: you'd soon come fast or damage your gear. Tom accordingly settled our gear on the edge of the bank at seventy fathoms, scraping round the edge of the bad ground – always home to the best pickings. It was late morning and everything was ready so once the gear was down I ascended to the bridge to keep Tom company.

I had worked this ground quite a few times before with different skippers and I was telling him about a few of its bad spots when a lone berg appeared directly in front of us. We'd been towing for less than an hour and dinner was fast approaching. 'The berg's almost certainly aground on the edge of the bank,' I advised the skipper, 'probably at seventy fathoms. You might well have to pull shoal to get past it rather than go deep into bad ground.'

Tom nodded and smiled condescendingly. 'Off you go,' he said. ' I'll see to it. Tell the cook to make me a meat sandwich. We'll haul straight after dinner.'

I sorted out the old man's snack, then went to the officers' mess and settled down to enjoy a nice plate of roast and veg. But barely halfway through my meal, the familiar sound of winch brakes screeching and trawl warps whizzing told me that once again the gear had come fast on the bottom. I left my dinner and made a quick dash to the drying-room for my oilskins. Although the weather was fine, we'd be bringing plenty of water aboard with the gear.

Out on deck we had already released the warps from the towing block, and the winchman was steadily heaving in 220 fathoms of warp. Our engines had stopped, so the ship was slowly being hove back to the fastener. We were barely past the iceberg, which was now astern of us. Just our luck to come fast so close to the berg, I thought. With each passing minute we were getting ever closer to this ice mountain, and the skipper had to use the engines to try to manoeuvre us clear. But by now the berg was towering above us. My God! Perhaps we'd come fast to the iceberg itself. Our new skipper makes his first Greenland tow and he captures a berg!

Tom must have ignored my words of advice and tried to pass outside the berg by slipping into the deeper water. Rather foolish, because you never know how deep an iceberg will reach.

Having now grasped the situation, I stopped the winch to give the skipper a chance to manoeuvre from side to side and try to work the gear free. Then I would call out to him and ask if we should slack some wire away, allowing him to move back round the berg and pull the gear out the way it went in. But before I had the chance, Tom demonstrated the other side of his nature. Dropping the bridge window, he leaned out, face twisted and purple with rage. 'Why the fucking hell have you stopped the winch, when we're trying to heave the gear free?' he screamed, 'Do you realise how difficult it is to handle the ship in these circumstances?'

This made no sense to me. Of course I realised how difficult it was. That's exactly why I was trying to give him room to manoeuvre. And this wasn't the last of Tom's outbursts. They seemed to occur every time he was under stress. Just as we were about to start heaving again, the skipper stuck his head out once more. 'I think it's the after warp that's fast. Unship that and heave on the fore warp.'

That finally did the trick, although not before we'd had a close shave with the ice. Once the gear was back aboard we found it undamaged, all except for the after Dan Leno. The large twenty-four-inch diameter steel bobbin was squashed flat as a penny. But that was all, quite amazing really. The crew decided that Tommy Tucker was a lucky fucker, especially as we took a bag of fish with it.

We put the gear down again and I returned to the bridge. Tom was back to his usual chirpy self – a veritable Jekyll and Hyde. 'By, I bet you were shitting y'self then,' he said.' You needn't have worried. I wouldn't have let us touch it.

'I was worried that we might strip the screw on an underwater shelf,' I replied. 'Maybe you haven't seen what can happen with these bergs. Sometimes a large piece breaks off underneath and alters the centre of gravity. Then the whole thing rolls over. If that had happened just now, it would have flipped us out of the water like a kid's rubber duck.'

'Nah, you worry too much,' grinned the skipper. 'You'd better get down the fish-room and make sure they're putting our first catch away properly. I'll see you later.'

Thankfully, Tom didn't try to repeat the tow. Instead he just kept moving down the edge of the bank towards the land. He wasn't bothered about the gunboat. The only one we knew of was based in Godhaab, the capital, about 700 miles to the north, although there was a spotter plane which could take pictures of us. We kept on towing towards the land, in weather about as good as I'd ever seen at Greenland, with light winds and occasional breaks in the clouds where the sun shone through.

We hauled about two miles off Cape Egede, as close as I'd ever been, and fetched up two slack bags of fish. As we were heaving the second haul down through the bellies and into the cod-ends by fleeting the net up with the bridge-top Gilson wire, Tom suddenly sang out to me.

'Hey, Bob! This isn't a little gunboat coming towards us, is it?'

I looked up. A small skiff driven by an outboard motor was about 150 yards away. With four Eskimos aboard, it was approaching at an angle and looking to pass ahead of us. I gave it a quick glance as we took the final heave that sent the fish down into the cod-end. 'Naw, it'll be a hunting party,' I said dismissively, turning back to the job. But as the narrow skiff came abreast of the bridge, about 100 yards off, the guy amidships suddenly raised what looked like a blunderbuss. He let fly over the wheelhouse, and a hail of shrapnel and metal bits came flying out of the trumpet-shaped barrel.

With a tinkle of the telegraph, the ship was immediately surging ahead again, even though we still had a bag of fish over the side. Tom was getting out of there as fast as he could, afraid they were after teaching him a lesson. The bag was now floating in the water, suspended from the Gilson block above the bridge. This small block was not designed to lift a bag of fish, even one as light as this. As the ship quickly gathered way, the sea washed the bag along the rail, knocking the bosun, who was closest to the action, right across the deck. Meanwhile we dragged the cod-end, now skimming over the water, alongside.

I looked up to protest, only to see a flight of ducks passing overhead, undoubtedly the target of our grinning hunters. The crew and I couldn't resist drawing Tom's attention to them as they flew by and the incident soon became the topic of some joking and leg-pulling. Still, it showed that our skipper had a dangerous tendency to over-react at times.

The rest of the trip went by without incident, though more by good luck than good judgment. Tommy still wouldn't heed my warnings about icebergs, alarming me on one occasion by electing to tow between two bergs that were very close together. I again pointed out that this pair were close enough to be joined together under the water. In the past, our radar had measured bergs over half a mile long, and these were less than a hundred yards apart.

But once again our skipper got away with it. You couldn't deny that TT was a good fisherman. Even though a spell of bad weather cost us a couple of days, he soon found us some good fishing and filled the ship up. As a result we steamed home again in good spirits, and the captain and I remained firm friends.

Our journey home was uneventful, but overloading at Hull Docks conspired to send us to Grimsby to discharge – news which made our skipper very morose. The reason was his half-brother, Randy Latus, who had apparently got into bad company and was now living in Grimsby with an unsuitable woman. Randy had once enjoyed good prospects – he had sailed with Tom some months before and was making excellent progress – until, that is, they landed in Grimsby. Randy had gone off with a girl there and wouldn't come back despite his family's protests. Randy by name and randy by nature apparently.

Now this latest news had stirred Tom up again. Still, he seemed resigned to leave matters alone this time.

We docked on the evening tide, so the lads had no chance to get home that night. By the time they'd caught the train to New Holland, they'd have missed the last ferry to Hull. Most of them decided to jump ashore instead and go into town for a few drinks. Again, I didn't join them because I knew I'd have to be up in the middle of the night to keep an eye on the fish, and Tom had decided to stop on board and sort out his bonded stores for the next trip. It was all very quiet with everyone ashore.

I was sitting in my berth sorting out the list of deck stores, when suddenly the skipper appeared at my door. While checking the bond locker, Tom had felt obliged to finish off some of the dregs and wanted me to join him. And what could I do but obey the skipper's orders? I dropped what I was doing and went up to his berth, rather more comfortable than mine – and, more importantly, closer to the locker. Before long we'd finished off the remaining few bottles, and the last of the whisky. Tom now decided it was too miserable on board on our own; he wanted to go visit one of his skipper friends in Grimsby. The guy owned a late night café and Tom insisted I go with him for moral support. We tidied ourselves up quickly and walked off the dock to find a taxi.

The skipper was a little ahead of me where the drinking was concerned, so it was no surprise when we stopped at the nearest pub, knocked back a couple more whiskys before time was called, and then stocked up with extra supplies. The taxi driver frowned a little when we threw three crates of beer in the back, but he said nothing and took us quickly to the café, the only blaze of light on Freeman Street at this time of night. Although just a simple place serving nothing but soft drinks and snacks, it was bouncing. Two little knots of policemen were standing almost directly opposite. That said it all.

There was no sign of Tom's skipper friend, but his wife was serving behind the little bar. 'Find a seat in one of the cubicles for a few minutes,' she said. 'I'll bring you a couple of coffees until I've time to come over and chat.'

We were lucky to find a couple of seats on one side of a cubicle opposite two rough-looking characters, each with two empty cola bottles in front of them. They looked a bit like Hank Marvin and Humphrey Bogard. Our coffees arrived quickly but Tom seemed uncomfortable. He was restless and impatient and kept looking towards the bar. Scanning the crowded room, I noticed the bosun sitting with a few of the lads in another cubicle. I caught his eye and we exchanged nods. Then the brute sitting opposite Tom suddenly leaned forward. 'Give us some of your coffee,' he said.

What a cheek. 'You really want some coffee?' Tom replied.

'Yes, I do.'

The table was only narrow, barely two feet separating us from our adversaries, and our little skipper leaned forward until his nose was nearly touching the other guy's. 'Then buy your own fucking coffee!' he roared.

The face of the bad 'un clouded over even further. Taking a deep breath, he leaned back and nudged his mate. 'Warn the gang behind us,' he muttered.

The ape in front of me then put his arm over the shoulder-high divider, nudged one of the four blokes in the cubicle behind him and gave him some sort of signal. Quick action was needed before we got a bottle across our heads. Stretching up, I caught the bosun's eye and waved him over. The bosun was heftily built and our new-found chums hesitated. 'Now then, I'm surprised to see you all in here,' I said, exaggerating somewhat. 'Looks like most of the crew's here.' I might perhaps have spotted a couple of others.

Now I had to find a good reason for calling him over. 'We've got a few beers in the cab. There might be one or two for you when we get back, OK?'

The bosun nodded affably. 'Great!' he replied. 'Thanks.' He had a quick word with skipper and moved off.

'Forget it. There's too many of 'em,' said Public Enemy Number One.

Result!

I was struggling to get Tom out of there before the lads made off. Then he suddenly remembered his half-brother and we were off like a shot out to the taxi. But, bosun apart, the rest of the lads had followed us – they must have heard about the beer. We were all completely sozzled and showed little respect for anyone. First the skipper jumped into the front seat of our taxi and started giving instructions; then a few of the lads tried to climb in the back with me. Our driver freaked out when they tried to duck down behind the seats under the noses of the policemen standing two yards from the door. I let in two of the crew, but the others had to jump into the taxi behind.

Tom directed us down some pretty dark and dingy streets in a rough part of town and we finally stopped outside a small mid-terrace in a narrow street. A light was shining behind the dirty net curtain in the downstairs room, and Tom jumped out and knocked on the door. 'Bring the booze,' he called over his shoulder.

His knock was answered by Randy, who was naturally pleased to see his brother and invited him in without quite grasping that he wasn't alone. I followed, and the two lads with us humped the beer in behind me. By now the second taxi had arrived and the other three lads joined us too. Randy made no objection; he was a pretty laid-back, easygoing sort of guy. But his girlfriend Stella – a slim, lithe, rather gaunt-looking girl in her early twenties – took a different view. With her deep-set eyes and pouting lower lip, Stella oozed sex appeal with every exaggerated movement as she danced in bare feet to music from a portable record-player.

It wasn't hard to see what had attracted Randy! However, Stella's glassy eyes told a different story, strongly suggesting that she was under the influence of some kind of intoxicant.

Taking some beers, the boys settled themselves down on the only furniture in the room – an old settee and matching armchair. Painted floorboards surrounded a square of carpet, and there was a nice fire going. We shared out the rest of the booze, and Tom, Randy and I moved into the back-kitchen, while Stella tried to dance with a couple of the younger lads. The kitchen was also pretty bare, nothing but the usual sink and draining boards, a cooker, a small rough wooden table and two small chairs. Dirty cracked mugs and chipped tumblers sticky with dregs littered the table. But most staggering of all was the orange-box nailed end up on the back wall to form a cupboard for condiments, its hinged lid used as a door. It hadn't even been painted.

Tom pulled a half bottle of whisky out of his pocket, while he and Randy held a heated discussion about coming back home. I took charge of the whisky, rinsing out a couple of the tumblers for Tom and his brother, and cleaning a tot glass more thoroughly for myself. As Tom became ever more abusive, I stood to one side, still trying to find the words to calm them down, but in so doing I absent-mindedly rested my hand on the orange-box cupboard.

Just then Tom referred to Stella as a slut. That really kicked things off and Randy started pushing Tom around. Stella overheard the rumpus and came rushing in, just as the orange-box collapsed onto the floor under the weight of my hand. 'Get out,' she screamed. 'You come into my house, abusing me and destroying my furniture. Get out!'

'Furniture?' said Tom.

This made me laugh, I just couldn't stop myself. Stella bounced a mug off Tom's forehead in reply, then dashed into the front room to chase the rest of the lads out of the place. Tom made to go after her in search of revenge but Randy seized hold of him and punches started to fly. I jumped in quickly to separate them, pushing our abusive skipper out the open back door, still trying to apologise to Randy and calm him down. But the pandemonium issuing from the front room was now so alarming that I had to head there first. It sounded like murder with all the screaming, shouting and smashing glass.

The scene that greeted me as I stepped into the room was quite incredible. It was a complete battlefield. Stella was crouched behind the easy chair in one corner lobbing beer bottles from a crate close by as if they were German hand-grenades. Meanwhile my shipmates were all tucked down behind the couch opposite as if it was some kind of bunker. Each side was deliberately smashing bottles against the wall opposite, with broken glass and beer raining down on the victims.

Shouting made no difference, so I had to nip in and grab our crewmen one at a time by the scruff of the collar and drag them out into the front passage with orders to shift smartly before the police arrived. When I returned to the back yard, Tom had Randy pinned up against the wall. The skipper was leaning his head against his brother's chest and both were weeping with remorse. Pulling Tom back, I could just make out a great patch of blood on Randy's chest. 'What have you done to him?' I enquired in horror.

Thankfully the blood had all come from Tom's head, now bleeding profusely. I was glad to get our captain out of there and back to the fish dock, where one of the lads helped me to get him aboard just as the lumpers were starting on the fish. Of course, it just had to be the guys I remembered from the *St Amant* a couple of months earlier, when I broke my hand and had the altercation with the fireman. The sight of me helping another damaged member of the crew served only to reinforce their opinion. They were obviously dealing with some maritime thug or modern-day pirate, a mate just looking for trouble.

CHAPTER 11

SQUEEZING THE LAST OUNCE

One more trip with Tom and I was told to sign off. Tom was stopping to take over the new ship, and another skipper and mate were taking over the *St Alcuin*. So much for the promotion I had been anticipating. It soon became apparent that the gaffers wanted me to join Tommy in the new ship for a couple of trips just to help set her up.

I had mixed feelings about this. While selection to take a new ship was undoubtedly a feather in your cap, it always meant problems and extra work, even with a skipper less excitable than Tom. Still, I put all my doubts to one side for the moment. Although the ship had been launched, it would not be fitted out for another two or three weeks so at least I had some time to enjoy myself.

My cousin Jerry had recently moved across the city to take up residence not far from us. He earned good money working hard on shifts at a local iron foundry and certainly liked a drink, so we started going out together. A large new dancing venue, the Locarno, had recently been built in the centre of town, and I happened to pass by one afternoon as I was crossing town with Jerry and his wife May. Although not yet officially open, two of its main doors were gaping wide so we decided to stroll in for a nosey.

The Locarno certainly was a pretty plush affair. With its large dance floor, wide upper balcony with tables, semi-circular revolving stage and a couple of bars, it was something extra. While we were admiring the fittings, a dapper little man approached us. 'Hello,' he said, 'I'm Ivor Kirchin, leader of the new resident big band. You look just the sort of people we'd like as members. I could sign you up right now if you're interested.'

He then went on to tell us about the Sunday Club, an exclusive first-floor bar. Membership rules would be strictly enforced up there so we'd need photo ID for that. Now Jerry was more of a drinker than a dancer, but this looked like a great place to go with good music and we agreed to join. The Sunday Club interested Jerry as well. Ivor closed the deal by offering us complimentary tickets for the first week and we made a date.

I hadn't seen any of my fishing friends for some time – our spells at home hadn't quite coincided – but the very next day I bumped into my pal Terry on Hessle Road. We exchanged the usual greetings. When did you get home? What ship? How much money did she make? When do you go away again? It turned out his family and friends were having a bit of a do at the Westfield Country Club to celebrate his sister's wedding. 'Would you like to join us?' he asked me. 'You know everyone after all.'

I accepted graciously, so that very evening Terry, his brother Kenny and I were in a taxi heading for the outskirts of town and the old buildings of the Westfield Club. A little more up-market than most, the Westfield was often frequented by fish merchants and skippers. And as we walked to our table, who should I see across the room but Sandra? She was sitting with friends, but I knew she would have spotted me.

We had a good night. After the meal there was an artiste who sang, then it was all clear for drinking and dancing. Eventually it was my turn to get the drinks in and I went up to the bar, where two girls were sitting cross-legged on high stools. One of them was Sandra, her split skirt showing quite a bit of leg. Crikey, that's a bit of a change in persona, I thought. I took my place just behind her and she immediately turned towards me. 'Well, hello stranger,' she sneered, voice low. 'What kind of beau are you, then? Have your way with me and then disappear for weeks on end.'

I was incredulous. Have my way? I seemed to remember it was the other way round. 'Sorry, Sandra. But you know what my job's like. Here today, away tomorrow.'

'Is that all you've got to say for yourself?'

"No! Look, let me get these drinks in. Then if your friend doesn't mind I'll come back later for a dance. I'll explain then. OK?'

As we slid around on the dance floor later in the evening, I tried to make my case. 'I'm not looking for a permanent relationship at this stage in my career,' I told her. 'I'd love to take you to the new Locarno Ballroom when it opens next week, though.'

Sandra seemed happy enough at this so I arranged for us to make up a foursome with Jerry and May.

Sandra must have been waiting for me when I arrived by taxi to pick her up – one ring of the doorbell and there she was. The Locarno was still only half full when we arrived, so we met up with Jerry and May and sat and had a drink together till things warmed up. Persuading the reluctant Jerry on to the dance floor was never easy, but he began to weaken when they started playing some jive, and May eventually coaxed him into performing some of the contortions he called dancing.

Pretty soon we needed a rest from our exertions. By now though, all the ground-floor seats and tables were taken so we had to move upstairs to the balcony. There we bumped into Sandra's friends from the Westfield and took a table next to them. Then my cousin's neighbours appeared – with a very attractive young lady in tow. Doug and Betty I knew well, but not so their friend. 'We're off to the Sunday Club bar to get a drink,' said Doug. 'Do you fancy joining us?'

Of course, the Sunday Club was members only. Thanks to Ivor Kirchin, no problem for Jerry, May and me. But Sandra wasn't a member. Nevertheless, the three of us decided to follow them up there. With all the crush around the bars, we were having trouble getting served on this level, and besides Sandra was in animated conversation with her friends. I went over to tell her what we were up to and promised to bring her back a drink.

These were still early days for the Locarno, and you had to show your photo ID for the Sunday Club, so there was plenty of room in the almost private bar. Doug and Betty were already at the bar, along with their mysterious friend, giving me a chance to study her for a minute as we approached. Average height, good legs, auburn hair and shapely lips, nicely made up and with a beckoning sheen to them – I could see all that a glance. But what really drew my attention were her soft, twinkling eyes.

'Now, Bob. I want you to meet Janet,' said Betty. 'I've told her all about you and she said she's keen to meet you if you're a dancer.' Janet blushed and lowered her eyes for a moment. 'We both go to the same dance school. We're part of a chorus line that appears in some of the local musicals.'

I certainly wouldn't mind seeing those legs in a chorus line, I thought.

I moved over to Janet and started chatting with her one-to-one. Although obviously intelligent, she seemed very naive in some ways. 'I'm a beauty consultant for a cosmetics company,' she said. So that explained the subtle make-up then. 'What do you do for a living?'

I was reluctant to mention my actual status. 'I'm a fisherman,' I said simply.

'A fisherman?' echoed Janet. 'My dad's not too keen on fishermen. You don't look like one!'

'No, well I left my net at home,' I quipped.

'So you're on trawlers, then?'

'Yes, I sail as mate.'

'What does a mate do?'

Could she really be a Hull girl? Where had she been all her life? A convent? 'A mate is second in command, on trawlers anyway,' I informed her.

'Ah well, maybe that explains your polite demeanour,' she responded graciously. She was certainly articulate enough.

'Listen, if you're so keen on dancing, how about I pick you up and bring you here next week?'

'Yes please,' she replied enthusiastically. 'It would be lovely to have someone escort me to a dance for a change.'

'Right,' I continued. 'If you've got a phone, perhaps I could give you a ring next week and arrange a date to suit us both. What's your number?'

Janet wrote the number on the back of one of her promotion cards and I put it in my back pocket. 'Can I buy you a drink? I have to get one for Sandra anyway and take her it back.'

'You're here with another girl?' Janet spluttered.

'Well, yes,' I replied, fingers crossed firmly behind my back. 'But she's not a regular girlfriend, more the friend of a friend. I've just come along as her partner for tonight.'

At least that was the way I saw it, though Sandra might have been thinking rather differently.

I bought the round and handed Janet her drink. 'It's been great meeting you. I'll look forward to seeing you next week. Bye!' Then off I went with the drinks, leaving Janet perplexed. I certainly was keen to meet up with her again.

Sandra's friends had only just left when I got back, so she wasn't too upset, just a little bit miffed that I'd taken so long. But she soon cheered up as we sipped our drinks, then we went down to rejoin Jerry and May on the dance floor below. No sign of Janet. Still, she might have been looking out for me, so I tried to keep my distance from my partner as I stared up at the thousand little lights in the ceiling above.

All in all Sandra and I both had a good night. I took her home in a taxi and once again the driver agreed to wait half an hour at the end of the drive while I walked her to the door. The lights were on, so someone was still up and about, and I certainly didn't relish meeting any of the family at this time of night. But I had no need to worry. Leading me down a path at the side of the house, Sandra took me across the huge garden to a little summer-house with a porch. There she swung open some French windows to reveal, just visible in the light from the house, a long, well-cushioned garden seat.

Pulling me down next to her, Sandra immediately put her arms around my neck and started a smooching session. She was clearly planning to arouse me in double quick time and in this, I have to confess, she was pretty successful. Lying down full length on this wide wicker couch was difficult to say the least, but we finally managed it – Sandra lying with her knees bent up, her lovely dance dress up around her waist, me kneeling with my trousers around my thighs.

Though hardly a bewitching union, it certainly was a lively one on Sandra's part. After saying goodnight, I walked back down the drive feeling somewhat less than satisfied, but certain that I'd find two bruises on my buttocks in the morning where Sandra had dug her heels in.

Next morning I slept late. With nothing pressing on the agenda I was intending to go to Sydney Scarborough, the well-known Hull record shop where you could 'try before you buy', listening to the records of your choice in one of their booths. It was a favourite place for fishermen, who could spend all morning like that, as long as they bought something in the end. But my father rang from the office to spoil my plans. 'Better start sorting out your gear and packing a bag for next trip. I want you to get up to Greenock and supervise the deck fittings as they finish off the ship. Better pack a full kit-bag. You'll be helping to sail her from there for trials at the end of the week, and you might not get back here before your first trip.'

This was all a bit sudden. More to the point, what was I going to do for pay? The ship wasn't yet ours so I couldn't be signed on articles. And I wasn't part of the shore staff so there was no provision for me to receive wages. Remember that, like any trawler skipper and mate, I was a share man. I didn't get weekly pay; any cash I received came from my share of the trip, normally three weeks long. Now I would be working for some time before the ship even sailed.

What on earth did they want me up there for anyway? We already had a manager from each department on site to supervise each section of the vessel. 'We need you to advise on the deck furniture,' said my boss. 'Nobody up there has any recent experience of the modern trawl, and it's changed so much. Different wire leads and block angles, that sort of thing. Otherwise you'll come back after the first trip wanting everything changing. These people have never built a *trawler* before you know.'

'And what will I do for money?'

'We've already ordered rail tickets for you. They'll be delivered to you along with some travel expenses and we'll book accommodation as well. My assistant's up there already. He'll meet you and advance you a sub if you need any more through the week.'

Of course, I should have picked up on that word advance. I simply assumed that my accommodation would provide some food and that I might be able to use the shipbuilder's canteen. But the phone went down abruptly and I'd no chance to ask any further questions. Father always tried to remain detached when he was talking company business.

The tickets arrived that afternoon along with a small amount of cash. My train left first thing in the morning, changing at Glasgow for Greenock, further down the Clyde. It had all been a bit of a rush, but I left the house carrying a kit-bag packed for a full voyage, an overnight bag with a couple of shore items, and some packing-up Mum had insisted on. It was a good job too because a meal on the train would have swallowed up all my travel expenses. I did have some money of my own, though I had earmarked that for entertainment during my time up there.

Then came an awful thought. I wouldn't be able to ring Janet. Her number was still in the back pocket of my other trousers. Never mind, I'd sort that out later. Right now I was contemplating a comfortable stay in a nice hotel. But reality proved a sore disappointment: a gallop down Glasgow's Sauchiehall Street laden with gear to catch my connection to Greenock, followed on my arrival by an escort to the Seamen's Mission!

We spent long days aboard the *St Giles*. There was much more to sort out all over the ship than I ever expected and everything had to be done at a rush to meet the delivery date. But it was all worthwhile. When the *St Giles* was finished she was the most graceful-looking trawler I had ever seen.

Then came another shock. The firm was only sending another three men up from Hull, making just four of us to man the vessel for speed trials on the Clyde, before taking her round to Fleetwood to store for her first voyage. Just four men to man a ship fore and aft and keep watches twenty-four hours a day. A bit demanding, sure, but as far as the owners were concerned we were only fishermen.

And we had to do all this in a severely overcrowded vessel. With almost forty people on board a ship built for a crew of twenty, and with accommodation for a maximum of twenty-five, we had to resort to what was known as hot-bunking. Almost everybody had to share a bunk, one turning in as another turned out.

By the time we reached Fleetwood all four of us were pretty worn out. Why Fleetwood? you might ask. Why not return to Hull? Well, the excuse was that Fleetwood was closer to Greenock and the fishing grounds. We could complete our fishing trials with the builders on board and then proceed on to either Greenland or Iceland. But Fleetwood was also Tom's home town and I think he played a big part in the decision.

To me, it was ludicrous. Supplying a brand-new ship takes a tremendous amount of gear and stores, what with three trawls (one in sections), ropes, steel bobbins, heaving wires, warps, cables, shackles and a host of other items, among them the engine room and cook's stores. It normally occupies several departments for a full week. On this occasion, there were just the four of us to load stores and put all the gear in place for fishing – and all apparently within forty-eight hours.

My old friend Hughie was chief engineer in this new ship and the two of us now faced a considerable headache. The skipper was hardly ever to be seen. As the Fleetwood lad he was too busy showing off his new ship to the local dignitaries. She certainly was a sight to behold, her ground-breaking, streamlined, elegant lines making her look more like a private yacht. But it was unfair of Tom to keep inviting groups of friends and officials on board for lunch or afternoon tea, when poor old Harry Price, the cook, already had all these extra mouths to feed and was still trying to stow his stores and utensils.

On our first day in Fleetwood, two lorries from Hull were due to bring us the three trawls plus the bobbins and ground gear. The remainder we would source from local companies. The rest of the crew were supposed to arrive even earlier by bus from Hull so they would be available for the unloading. The lorries turned up as expected, but not so the crew. They didn't arrive until ten, and even at that time in the morning they'd managed to find themselves some drink. They weren't exactly drunk, but they were pretty merry.

By the time they'd sorted themselves out and unloaded one lorry of net it was lunchtime. 'We'll get them back within the hour,' promised the two ship's runners escorting them. But that didn't happen either. The bosun was a Fleetwood lad, along with five of the ten crewmen, and they all went into a club to meet up with old friends. Only half the crew returned, my original three deckies plus two others. Wonderful!

The two runners were keen to get back to Hull, but I had other ideas. They were going nowhere till they helped me to retrieve my crew. The runners directed the bus back to the club and in we went to try and coax our deckies away from their friends. Mind you, coaxing is putting it mildly. Given the amount they'd been putting away, I had to get a bit belligerent with some of the boys and that didn't go down too well with their mates. To them I was just a Yorky interloper.

A time-consuming struggle ensued, but eventually we had most of the crew back on the bus. The bosun, however, was a problem. He wouldn't leave without his half of beer, while the doorman wouldn't let the glass out of the club. I closed the argument by digging down into my pocket for the price of a pint, or to pay for the glass – I wasn't hanging around to find out which. I hurried the bosun on to the bus, only to find it was now the turn of the bus driver to turn awkward. 'I'm not moving until he's supped up,' he said. But the bosun wanted to take his time ... And to think there was plenty more to come!

We had already wasted a lot of time, and back aboard the *St Giles* I found it hard to motivate a mostly glassy-eyed crew. We still had the other lorry to unload, and a trawl to put together and alongside ready for the fishing trials. One of the local fishing companies had been charged with supplying our ironware – shackles, axes, slip hooks, beckets and the like. There was plenty to move and they were tackling the job by filling a hand-cart with the stuff, wheeling it to the quayside above us, and shooting it on to the fore-deck for my gang to shift, ready or not. The ironware was already obstructing the men assembling the trawl and there were at least another three or four cartloads to come.

'Can't you stop this while the deck's littered with net and wires?' I shouted to the foreman.

He spread his hands wide and shrugged his shoulders. 'I've a job to do,' he replied.

'I don't care,' I shot back. 'Don't unload any more until you've cleared it with me.'

Before we had time to pursue our discussion, Hughie appeared. 'The bonded stores are on board,' he said. 'The skipper's not here to sign for them so the customs guy wants you to check them over with him and watch them put under seal.'

So off I went aft with Hughie. He was worrying about some forty-gallon drums of lubricating and diesel oil. They were destined for the storage tanks in the engine room but had been dumped on the boat deck instead. 'I don't know how I'm going to move them,' he said. He had other problems too, but he said no more. He knew that we were both under pressure.

The uniformed customs officer was inside the steel-doored, walk-in bonded store, waiting for us to check the tobacco, cigarettes and spirits on the shelves. I looked them over and signed his document. Then he took out his sealing wax and tape and locked the door. But he had nowhere to tie his seal – the door and the jamb had no eyelets or lugs. 'I can't leave the door unsealed,' he told me. 'You'll have to send the bonded stores back ashore until you've rectified things.'

Oh no! We couldn't handle that kind of delay in the time we had left to us. I turned to Hughie. 'Couldn't we just drill a small hole in the door and one in the jamb and pass the tape through?' I asked him.

'OK by me,' said the customs officer.

'Sorry,' said Hughie. 'I can't make any changes to the construction while the ship's in port. Only the shore people can organise that.'

By now I was getting frantic. Things were getting fraught on deck and I needed to get out there quickly. The crew weren't used to working non-stop on the day they joined a ship, especially on a job they thought rightly belonged to other people. 'Listen, Hugh,' I said. Have you got a drill that'll go through this steel?'

'Sure.'

'Then bring it here, please. I'll sort this out.'

Hughie nodded and sped away, aware that time was at a premium. In the interval, one or two deckies wandered off the deck into the galley for a drink and I chased them out. 'We're all stopping for a drink in half an hour,' I told them.

Hugh came back with a large drill and an electric lead. Having located a socket, I raised the drill to the door and was poised to start work when a foreman from the shore gang came wandering along the alley-way.

'You're not supposed to do that,' he warned me. 'If you start that drill my lads will go on strike.'

I looked over my shoulder at him. Hughie was staring at me, attempting to hide a grin. We'd sailed together many times before and he knew me well. 'Well, fucking strike then,' I snapped, and started up the drill.

I pressed on. From what I had seen, a strike by the shore gang would have little effect on us. And even if it did, it might bring the skipper and the assistant manager back to take charge. The foreman glowered for a minute then stormed off issuing various threats. The job was soon done and the officer passed his tape through the holes, sealing the door with wax and stamp. As I took the ship's share of the paperwork, Hughie gathered up the tools. 'I'll enjoy seeing you keel-hauled tomorrow,' he joked.

Back out on deck, I was just in time to see the hand-cart retreating from another small mountain of metal on the fore-deck, this time intended for the iron foundry store. I ran towards the fast-disappearing store-keeper. 'Do that again and I'll punch you on the nose,' I threatened him.

Just then the bosun sidled up. 'I think you need a break,' he suggested. 'Come on down with us.'

I had to agree. I was definitely becoming a macho mate.

While we were drinking our tea and scoffing the buns Harry had saved for us, the driver of a flat-back lorry came into the mess. 'I've got four half-ton trawl doors waiting,' he told me. 'You'll need to lift them off with your derricks.' My head was reeling. Something had gone badly wrong here. Given the height of the quay, our derricks wouldn't clear the lorry. We needed a mobile crane.

'The skipper's on board,' said Harry helpfully, putting his head through the serving-hatch. 'He's in the officers' mess.'

Right, I thought. Now's the time to get him involved. He can organise this.

Leaving my drink unfinished, I hurried along amidships to the officers' mess, where Tommy and friends were sitting with half a dozen beers in front of them. The skipper was on his way to fetch some more glasses as I walked in, and I stopped him in the alley-way outside. I started to explain the latest problem. 'Don't bother me with trivialities,' he replied, attempting to brush me to one side.

'Trivialities!!' I exploded, grabbing at his jacket as he walked by. 'Trivialities! You call all this trivial.'

But Tom didn't want a confrontation. Shrugging me off with another swing of the arm, he dashed for the stairway to his accommodation. 'Get back to work and do your job,' he shouted.

I chased after him, mad with rage. 'Do my job!' I bellowed. The skipper ran up the steps and straight into his berth, locking the door behind him. I followed and banged on the beautifully polished wood. 'It's about time you got out here and started doing *your* job, instead of showing off to all and sundry.'

'Get off this deck,' Tom shouted back. 'You're sacked.'

'No need to sack me,' I screamed in my turn. 'I've resigned.'

A hand came to rest gently on my shoulder. 'Whoa, Bob. Whoa. Calm down. This won't do any good.' It was Stan, the assistant manager. 'Stand back,' he told me, knocking on the skipper's door and shouting of him to open up.

Eventually Tom came out to face us, spluttering his protests. But Stan raised a hand to silence him. 'Now listen, you two,' he snapped. 'Tom, you can't sack him. And Bob, you can't resign. You were chosen by the owner to take this ship on its maiden voyage. He'd wash his hands of the pair of you if he heard you were countermanding his orders.' He gave us a chance to absorb this. 'So Bob,' he continued, 'tell me the problem and we'll sort it before I get the sack as well.'

Stan promised his help with all the hassles I'd encountered and sent me about my business. 'You're on rocky ground, you know,' he was telling Tom as I left. 'The owner's in Hull now, but he's due back on board in time for the fishing trials the day after tomorrow.'

That evening I went late for my evening meal. It had been a very long day. The captain, the sparks and the second engineer had been and gone, so the chief and I were the only takers for the second sitting in the little officers' mess. However, we were soon joined by another shattered man, Harry the cook.

I looked across at Hughie, red face still perspiring as he slumped down on the seat locker opposite me. 'What a fucking day,' he gasped. 'I don't know how they expect the four of us to cope with all the stuff we've had pelted at us down the engine room. There's little enough room as it is without all the drums and kegs and spares I've got to find space for. And that new switchboard is a nightmare.'

'I know the feeling,' I moaned. 'They're expecting too much. There's only nineteen of us after all. I've left one man out of course.'

'Yeh, I heard you and the old man had a fall-out,' grinned my old friend.

'Apparently we've been dealing with nothing but trivia,' I said, dismissing Hughie's comment with a flap of my hand. 'But we'll say no more about that.' Just then the bulkhead speaker crackled into life with some country and western. The sparks must have been trying out his new equipment. 'And what about you, Harry?' I continued sympathetically. 'You've had an exhausting day too. Dozens of meals to provide and just you and the lad to do it.'

Harry Price was a heavy-built man in late middle age, his crinkly hair now greying. Normally smart in appearance, he had once been a proper chef and was a cut above the average cook. He lived with his sister and was a bit too naive for shipboard life. 'I just don't know how I've coped!' he spluttered, mopping his brow with a sponge cloth from the galley. 'I've a mountain of work still to do, as well as this lot to clear away. You should see the galley. I've had to stack dirty pans and trays in every corner. That poor youngster is knackered; he isn't used to this amount of work. I'll have to shift most of this lot myself.'

Over the speaker, Harry's namesake, Ray Price, had burst into 'Heartaches by the Number, Troubles by the Score'. Hughie and I looked at each other, giggling sleepily, but we managed to control ourselves. 'Never mind, Harry,' I said. 'Hugh and I will clear this lot and carry it aft for you.'

'That'll be a help,' sighed the distraught cook. 'It's all the other stuff, though. I'll be at it till midnight. How do *you* cope, anyhow? You've half a lung missing and you're always flat out all day. Does the doctor give you special tablets to give you a boost?'

This last remark took me aback. How did Harry know? No one had mentioned my operation for a couple of years now. And why did he think that doctors could or would supply me with something to help me do my job?

'My sister's a surgeon's secretary, and she reckons they can prescribe booster tablets to give you extra strength,' continued the portly pan-shaker. 'He has some among his medicines. She showed me them. Yellow they were, but they're kept under strict control. After all, they're powerful stuff. Have you got any, Bob?'

It all sounded a bit far-fetched to me. His sister must have got it wrong. But I decided to play along just for fun. 'You're right,' I said, 'but don't tell anyone. I'm not supposed to have them unsupervised.'

Unseen by Harry, Hughie leaned back and grinned. But his smile faded when he saw that I was apparently serious. Surely he knew me better than that.

'I thought as much,' said Harry. 'Do you think you could let me have one?'

'Oh no, I can't do that,' I replied. *Especially as I didn't have any.* 'The doctor only let me have them on condition I keep a tight rein on 'em.'

Now Hughie's eyebrows were raised. This was news to him.

'Please, Bob,' pleaded Harry. 'I know you shouldn't but I really need something to help. Just this once.'

'Sorry, Harry. I daren't. You know how powerful they are.'

'Couldn't you just show us one?' said our suspicious chief.

Thanks, pal. I did my best to get out of it but the pair of them continued to pressure me. It was a case of deliver or back down ignominiously. 'OK,' I found myself saying, 'I'll just nip across to my berth and get one.'

Thinking feverishly, I slipped out of the dining cabin and across the alleyway. All I had was a little bottle of Yeastvite, which you could buy off the shelf of any chemist or big store. Advertised as a pick-me-up, they were mustard-yellow in colour and handy for headaches. I grabbed one and scrutinised it. Would it be good enough to fool my mates? I doubted it.

Returning to the mess, I laid the tablet on the palm of my hand.

'It's a bit smaller than the ones I've seen,' said Harry.

I had to think quickly. 'Yes, they've made them a bit more compact,' I replied.

'Let's have a look.' Harry reached out for the tablet.

'Best not,' I said, quickly withdrawing my hand.

'Why not?' Harry was hurt. 'You know my hands are clean.'

'I know. Still, I'd rather other people didn't handle my pills.'

'Surely it doesn't matter if it's Harry that's going to take it,' said the impish chief, eyes glinting with mischief.

'But he's not going to, is he?'

'Why not?' continued Hughie. 'I'm sure you could spare him one.'

'Oh please, Bob,' said Harry. 'Be a pal. I won't forget it if you do.'

Eventually I relented. 'OK then,' I said, shrugging my shoulders. 'But take it now before anyone else sees it.'

I handed the tablet to the eager cook, who took one final look before swilling it down with the remains of his tea. 'It's definitely not as bright a yellow as the ones my sister showed me.'

'Perhaps they've got a bit damp in my drawer,' I muttered in reply.

'Well, better get on before it gets any later,' said Harry, regaining his feet a little more enthusiastically. He collected the remains of the food from the hot cupboard and stumbled out down the passage to the galley, leaving Hugh and I to clear up for him.

'Now, what was going on there?' asked the chief. 'Was that for real or what?'

Arms folded, I looked at him with disgust. 'Of course it wasn't. All the years we've sailed together, have you ever known me take tablets?'

'No, but you were so convincing.'

'If I'm playing a part, I'm playing a part. It was just a bit of fun. You weren't much help, though.'

Hughie chuckled. 'Well I don't suppose it'll do him any harm. What was the tablet anyway?'

'A Yeastvite.'

'A Yeastvite?'

'Yes.'

'What are they for? Headaches? Or are they to help you to relax?'

'Something like that,' I said. 'Come on. Let's clear this stuff for him. He won't get any more help tonight. I've got paperwork to do.'

'Me too,' moaned Hugh. 'Oil and stores figures. Ugh.'

Hugh and I carried the stuff through to the galley. It looked like a scrapyard in there, dirty pans and trays stacked everywhere. Hands deep in the big sink, up to his arms in suds, Harry treated us to a big grin as we placed yet more work on the side for him. We smiled bashfully in return and scuttled off to our respective cabins.

An hour and a half later, my lists completed, I headed for the bathroom. No toilet roll, so I went aft to find out where the bosun had stowed them, passing the galley on my way. It was now immaculate. Harry had even filled a bucket with soapy water and was scrubbing down the bulkheads with a hand-brush! But we were on a new ship! And he'd told us he was shattered!

I collected a couple of rolls off the bosun and retraced my steps. There was Harry, still on his own, still scrubbing everything in sight! The chief's berth was just up the alley-way from mine. 'Hey, come and have a look at this,' I beckoned him. 'Come and see a shattered man in action.'

Putting my finger to my lips, I led the way as we tiptoed down the passage and peeped round the galley door. Harry was half buried in one of the ovens, wiping it down. Hughie pulled back in amazement. 'At this time of night? It looks like he's energy to burn.'

'Well, he's superman now, isn't he?' I grinned back.

'Yeh, but that's a tremendous amount of work to get through when you could be in bed. What did you actually give him?'

'What do you mean, actually give him? I've told you what they are. Come on, I'll show you.' I took my old pal to my berth, brandished the labelled bottle and shook out some pills.

'Bloody hell!' he spluttered. 'The power of suggestion, eh. Or are these tablets more potent than you think?'

'I've never seen them have an effect like that before,' I replied. 'They've cleared up the odd headache but that's all. Any more than that and I'd be making money out of them. Now I know what I need to rejuvenate me.' I pointed to the narrow bunk beside me. 'It's over there.'

'Fair enough, Rob. I think I'll stretch out too. I might read for a bit before I switch my light out. See you tomorrow.'

I also laid back with a magazine to have a little read before bedding down. It was only nine o'clock, but I was so tired that it wasn't long before the mag fell on my chest. I woke a couple of hours later with a dry mouth and made my way to the galley to fetch a drink, passing the cook's berth on the way. The door was wide open and the light still on. Glancing inside, I found Harry laid on his bunk reading, still dressed, looking smart and neat, hair nicely groomed and feet resting on a cushion. His legs must have been aching but he was still wide awake.

I ventured a word. 'Now then, Harry. You *still* awake?'

'Yeh, I can't sleep. That tablet was magic. I'm still feeling lively.'

'Mmmm,' I muttered. 'They don't last forever, though. You've had a long day and it's an early start tomorrow. Best get some rest now.'

Retracing my steps, I noticed that the chief's door was ajar on the hook. His light was still on so I couldn't resist peeping inside for a word. Hughie had also fallen asleep over his book, but he opened his eyes when he heard the door go. 'You old fellas should be tucked up properly this time o'night,' I jibed.

'Don't worry. I'll last out as long as you.'

'But not as long as our cook,' I said. 'Go and check him out.'

Back in my berth, I closed the door, stripped off, got into bed properly and switched off the light. A few minutes later I heard a knock at the door and Hughie peered in. I knew he must have followed my advice.

'Hey, Bob!' he asked, without turning on the light. 'You wouldn't have a couple of those tablets to spare, would you?'

'Not now, Hugh,' I mumbled drowsily. 'You'd never get off to sleep.'

The following day – with our fishing gear finally prepared and all the observers, engineers and technicians back on board – we sailed out on the tide. We were only supposed to go twenty or thirty miles out to put our gear on the bottom and make sure it would shoot away properly, checking that nothing hung up and that all the wires ran cleanly through the sheaves, blocks and bollards. But Tommy had other ideas and took us out rather further than planned. I could just imagine him telling the folk crowding the bridge that he'd catch them some nice hake or lemon sole to take home for tea. Eventually the gaffer started getting restless at this time-wasting, so we shot short, hit rough ground (thanks, Tom!) and soon came fast on the bottom.

We knocked the warps out the towing block and started to haul. Tom had trouble manoeuvring the ship, probably because of the crowded bridge, and before long we'd parted a cable, finishing up with a one-ended job. All this heavy gear hanging on only one wire. Just perfect! It would take us at least two hours to bring it all aboard. The shore people sailing with us found it quite a revelation when we eventually had the taffled trawl hung up on the various wires. For the lads and me though, it was just another exhausting day. I earned plaudits for the way I manoeuvred the gear on board, but they fell on deaf ears. My only interest was in getting rid of all these spectators as quickly as possible.

I was fast becoming demoralised; nothing was going according to plan. I'd been working on this ship for a week and a half already and I hadn't earned any money yet – and we were still nowhere near the fishing grounds. When we finally got clear we set off for Iceland. The lovely, yacht-like lines of the *St Giles* drew a lot of admiring comments, but we returned with an unexceptional trip on board – certainly not enough to recompense us for all the extra work we'd put in. In an effort to make up, we decided on Greenland for our next excursion. The trip out was uneventful, although the field ice that enveloped us from time to time soon rubbed off all the beautiful gloss paint used by the Scottish builders on the hull. But once we'd got the gear down there was plenty of fish, the weather stayed fine and we caught a good trip.

However, our luck didn't extend as far our journey home. A north-easterly gale sprang up and racing seas pounded the port side, washing off all the mock wood graining around the casing. All in all, we looked pretty shabby for a new vessel returning for only the second time to its home port. The heavier paint they used in Hull would soon put that right, though.

As far as I was concerned I'd done my bit. We had made all the changes required and successfully established our new vessel into the fleet, so I asked for a transfer. To my surprise, it was granted without question. Or, at least, they signed me off immediately to await a new appointment.

CHAPTER 12

THE OLD MAN

Although glad to be at home for a while I was more than a little concerned. After turning my nose up at a new ship, I might be given the walk-around for a month or more. I didn't think my father would allow it, but if I'd upset the old gaffer you never knew. Anyway, I decided to try to obtain what was known as the Greenland Ticket, which required me to submit six sextant sights to the Nautical School. It would be difficult to work these out on paper, and to set them out as positions on a chart. But if they were accepted I would receive an endorsement to my skipper's ticket allowing me to take a fishing vessel anywhere in the world.

I also wanted to renew my acquaintance with Janet. I tried ringing her on the number she'd given me, without success. 'She's unavailable,' said her mother, when I asked to speak to her daughter. Now that suggested that Janet didn't want to talk to me, probably because I hadn't rung as promised. Unaware of the demands made of a fisherman, she wouldn't know I'd been whisked away to Scotland and beyond. I had to think of a way to get in touch and explain things to her. I really was taken with the girl. She excited me.

Next day I went to visit Mr Harvey, the tutor for skippers and mates. He acted as examiner for the Greenland Ticket and I presented him with some of the sights I'd taken while steaming to the fishing grounds. I had more than the six needed in total, but there was a problem. Only two of them were star sights when three were required. However, Mr Harvey was impressed with my work and sympathetic when I explained the difficulty of obtaining star sights in the Arctic, where mist or total darkness nearly always obscures the horizon used to measure the angle. 'If you're bright enough to work out a sight backwards from an imaginary position,' he suggested, 'I'll include it in my assessment.' That seemed like a good idea and I went away intending to do just that over the next week.

Meanwhile cousin Jerry had been in touch again. Would I like to contribute to a party he was organising that evening at his place? I had done this before and they were pretty wild affairs. I could afford to donate most of the cash, and in return he let me take whoever I wanted and catered for *my* taste in food and drink. He named some of the people he was inviting. 'Sounds great,' I said. 'Some pretty girls in that lot.' He also mentioned Doug and Betty, his former neighbours, and I latched on to this straight away. 'Can you persuade them to bring their friend Janet?' I asked him. 'Maybe without mentioning me.'

'Sure,' he replied.

I contacted my shore-based friend Geoff, who always loved a party and had accompanied me on a few escapades in the past. I liked things to warm up a bit first so we decided not to arrive too early. I also wanted to make sure that Janet got there before I did. Geoff and I went to a club for a few drinks and immediately got chatting to two pretty girls who seemed very keen to link up with us. In fact, I was making good progress with one of them. But I decided that things were getting rather too tempting and quickly made our excuses.

My cousin now lived in a council house on an east Hull estate and on our way over I picked up a bottle of my favourite drink, Glayva liqueur. Things sounded to be in full swing when I knocked on the door. I was expecting Jerry or May to answer, but no. The door was opened by a young lady unknown to me. She had a glass in her hand, a cheeky smirk and a flirty attitude.

'Who are you?' she asked.

She knew perfectly well who I was, but never mind. 'I'm from next door,' I replied. 'I've come to complain about the noise.'

'I don't think so. The neighbours are here.'

'They're imposters. Anyway, I've brought this.' I held out the Glayva.

'I don't drink it. You can still come in, though.'

Then May's voice came from within. 'It's Rob,' she shouted. 'You'd better let him in.'

I stepped into the small hallway and then on into a crowded living-room. A few couples were sitting round listening to music and chatting, and some of the girls were passing drinks. But the first person I set eyes on was Janet. Her face registered a brief flash of surprise when she looked up and saw me. Then she glanced sideways at Doug and Betty, realisation dawning that she had been the subject of a conspiracy.

Geoff made his way into the back-kitchen. He knew my cousin, and it was natural for him to gravitate towards the booze. I headed straight for Janet to make my peace. I had to tell her what had happened nearly two months before. Janet was sitting on a stool next to the fireplace, Betty was in the armchair next to her and I perched on the arm between the two. I greeted Betty, then turned all my attention on Janet. 'I was whipped away to Scotland to join a new ship,' I explained. She was obviously weakening. 'Then we headed straight off to Iceland. I didn't think you'd get so upset over one missed phone call.'

'I'm not used to being snubbed and I was so disappointed. I'd been really looking forward to it.' My heart jumped. Fancy her caring so much.

Sharron, the girl who had opened the door, now came fussing across, offering to get me a drink. As she was serving other people as well, I requested my usual whisky and lemonade. She said nothing to Janet, though.

'Could you top up this g & t for Janet as well, please,' I asked. This made Jan relax even more. She was definitely warming to me. Her eyes were sparkling and she was laughing at my jokes. Then Jerry announced that we were going to play party games as usual.

Charades came first, lots of fun until we became too good at guessing them. We were told to pair up for the next game so naturally Janet and I decided to stay together. We had to stand face to face, hugging each other while someone tethered us ankle to ankle and tied our hands loosely behind our partner's back. Our bodies were pressed so close together you couldn't get a cig paper between them. And Janet and I still hadn't danced together yet, never mind kissing. Jan giggled a lot, clearly a little embarrassed by it all. She wouldn't look me in the face, fixing her eyes on Betty or May as she turned her head or looked over my shoulder.

The game was a sort of race. Moving sideways or back and forth, you had to step over articles or burst balloons and finish before your opponents. We nearly fell over a couple of times, producing plenty of laughs, but Jan lost a lot of her inhibitions as the game went on and we just managed to win. Only now did she look up at me, face flushed and grinning with delight.

We got another drink and sat close together while we watched the others taking their turn. I was in seventh heaven. Then came the next game. This time we had to stand back to back with legs apart, bend down and touch our toes. Janet had no inkling of what was about to happen next. Two ladies knelt down, made us reach between our legs and grasp each other by the hand, then tied our hands together. Now they set us off on the same routine as before, sending those hands right up against our partner's upper thighs and crotch.

Janet continued to shriek and giggle at every attempt to reach our goal. I can only imagine what was going through her mind! I certainly wasn't expecting to find my hands so far up her thigh this early in our relationship! We lost the game, and the way Jan kept smoothing her dress down front and back made it obvious she was feeling rather embarrassed, wondering if she might have exposed rather more than she wanted to.

To add to the fun we were instructed to change partners for the next couple of games. Before I could select anyone else, Sharron had appeared in front of me, so that was soon settled. The games continued in similar vein, Sharron participating with enthusiasm, clearly loving every minute. Fine by me, I was flattered by her evident interest.

Janet had partnered up with Doug and they were deep in conversation when we stopped for eats. Sharron pulled me out into the kitchen, showing me the bacon bones and other titbits I'd requested, then made sure I had a glass of Glayva. She too had a drink in her hand but found every excuse to put her free arm around my neck and pull me close. Then she pushed me down onto a kitchen chair and sat on my knee. The Glayva and other drinks were definitely taking effect. I had my arm around Sharron's waist and was in merry mood.

I must have been in there longer than I realised. Suddenly Janet entered the room and walked up to me. 'I just thought I'd let you know I've ordered a taxi,' she said. ' I'm going now.' And with that she swept out of the room.

Mumbling my excuses, I humped Sharron off my knee and chased after Janet. She was outside by the time I caught up with her and a little bit cool when I approached. 'I thought you were enjoying yourself,' I said. 'Why are you leaving so soon?'

'Because I want to,' she replied. 'Anyhow, I don't want to leave it too late.'

'Well, I hope it's not because of me. I haven't done anything to upset you, have I?'

'No, how could you? You've spent most of your time in another room with another girl?'

I'd hardly spent *most* of my time with another girl, surely. But just then the taxi arrived. 'Well at least let me escort you home,' I insisted, and followed her into the car.

Inside the taxi I snuggled up close. 'It's been great meeting up with you again,' I told her. Jan mellowed a bit as we drove across town, reassured by my readiness to leave the party to see her home. I was very aware of her subtle perfume and the warmth of her body during the quiet spells and vowed to do what I could to maintain the relationship.

Janet lived in a council house down a cul-de-sac on the edge of town. 'Can I see you again?' I asked, when the car stopped. 'There's a Doris Day film on at the Dorchester. Would you like to go tomorrow night?'

To my delight she agreed. I arranged to pick her up just after seven and she scampered off into the house. Next day I submitted my false star sight to Mr Harvey at the Nautical School and thought about the evening to come. I had decided to pick Janet up in my car as we wouldn't be drinking. During a successful run with Skipper Farguson I had bought myself a brand new car, a powder-blue Ford Consul 375. It had a bench seat in the front and the 375 style made it look quite streamlined.

When I knocked at her house, Janet opened the door straight away. Out she stepped, quickly closing the door behind her. Was she trying to stop her mum and dad catching sight of me? If so, she failed. I was sure I saw the curtain twitch as we walked down the path. Then Jan caught sight of the car. 'Wow!' she gasped. 'Who's is that? Is it your dad's?'

'No, he's got a Triumph Herald. That's mine. It's straight from the factory, all bought and paid for.'

'Gosh,' she said. 'How long did it take you to save up for it?'

'A while.'

Jan obviously didn't know how much a trawler mate could earn and I wasn't going to enlighten her. I helped her on to the nice wide front bench seat and she leant back, preening herself and grinning broadly as she glanced back towards the house.

'What do your mum and dad think about you going out with a fisherman, then?' I asked as I climbed in.

'I don't think Dad's too keen but Mum did say what a nice voice you have.'

Oh good, I was making some progress then.

Having parked up in a nearby street, we cut through a passage directly opposite the large, square cinema frontage, with its line of glassed double-doors protected by a built-in canopy. The seats were plush and I paid extra to sit at the back. It was a typical Doris Day musical comedy and during a love scene I slid my arm along the back of Jan's seat. She made no objection and even leant in to me for the rest of the film.

Coming out after the picture, I made my usual move. 'Would you like a look at the river before I take you home?' I asked. Once again Jan didn't demur, so we drove out on to Victoria Pier overlooking the Humber. The Humber ferry was moored nearby, tied up for the night to its pontoon, and the area was pretty quiet. I switched on the radio and we looked out across the water at the lights of the vessels plying up and down the river. It was quite romantic really with the water sparkling in the moonlight.

As I snuggled up to Janet, Jimmy Young was singing 'Unchained Melody'. '*I hunger for your touch*,' he crooned, and I knew exactly what he meant. Pulling Jan towards me, I gave her a long, gentle kiss. She hummed appreciatively and I continued to rub my lips against a spot just beneath her ear. She sighed deeply, almost sobbing now, and I broke off for a while before gently turning her head towards me for another kiss. Then I allowed my hand to slide down under her jacket and inside her blouse, poking my finger-tips under the strap of her brassière.

'Please don't, Rob,' she said softly in my ear. 'We hardly know each other.'

Her words affected me more than any possible action on her part. I respected her enormously and complied immediately with her wishes. But I desired her as well, and the hot blood in my veins would ensure I tried again soon.

We regained our composure and I took Jan home. 'Would you like to go dancing at the Locarno again?' I asked before she left me.

'I'd love to.'

'Great. I'll contact Jerry and May to join us. If that's all right with you?'

'It would be fine.' She gave me a kiss, just a quick one in case anyone was watching. Then she was gone.

The next morning I rose full of the joys of life, remembering the night before and looking forward to the weekend to come. I would contact Jerry after he finished work and I'd retrieved my papers from the Nautical School. They had already let me know my figures were correct and they were ready to endorse my brand-new Skipper's Ticket.

I was getting ready to leave when the telephone rang. 'Get yourself down to the office for eleven o'clock to see the boss,' said my father. 'You're taking the St Keverne and she sails tomorrow.' The phone went down and that was it! I was going skipper of one of the big 'uns.

My mind was in a whirl. I'd have to get my kit-bag packed in a hurry, then have my bag of deck gear and waterproofs put on board. Hang on a minute. I wouldn't need deck gear because I wouldn't be on deck! In fact, I didn't even need a kit-bag. Skippers rarely used one, just a case for the lighter stuff they needed for the bridge, like slacks and warm shirts. But I hadn't time to do anything much now. I had to get ready to meet the gaffer.

Mounting the extra flight of stairs to the owner's panelled office was more thrilling than intimidating. I had met the big boss two or three times lately when he'd come in to see the manager while I was receiving instructions. And, of course, he knew of my achievements as mate. The boss came out from behind his desk and shook my hand, inviting me to take a seat in front of him. I perched on the edge of the padded chair. 'Which grounds have you been to?' he began. 'And where do you have the most experience?'

I told him what I'd been doing.

'I'm giving you a couple of trips in one of the bigger ships to begin with,' he continued. 'I want to give you every opportunity to succeed. Bigger ships have greater expenses, of course. So you'll need to catch more fish to meet them. Where would you like to go for your first trip?'

'Iceland,' I replied. 'Some of the banks are difficult to work but they offer more scope and the fish there is of such high quality.'

'Iceland it is, then. Best of luck.' And he stood and shook my hand again.

I returned to the manager's office thinking that I might get at least two trips in the Keverne. There I was asked what trawl fittings I wanted putting aboard, but otherwise I was quickly despatched to the bonded stores to order the duty-free for the ship.

I chased about a lot that day. There was so much I needed to do. I hadn't even found out who was going to be my mate. I wasn't so bothered about the rest of the crew – in a ship of this class they'd be company regulars. But my second in command had to be someone I could get along with. The day flew by and I still had my case to pack. Suddenly I realised that I wouldn't be home at the weekend to take Janet to the dance. Even though it was getting late I knew I had to get in touch and explain why.

Janet sounded enthusiastic when her mother called her to the phone. But her mood quickly grew subdued when I told her we wouldn't be able to see each other for another three weeks.

'I'm afraid it'll be even longer than that, Rob,' she moaned. 'The company's sending me to London on a course in about three weeks.'

'Oh dear,' I replied, 'it *will* be much longer, then. We're only going to Iceland but I don't think we can make it home any sooner at this time of year.'

'You're going to Iceland?'

'Yes, I am.'

'And you're taking the ship there?'

'Yeh!'

'Are you sure you know the way?' Jan sounded rather concerned.

This amused me so much that I couldn't resist winding her up a little. 'Not really,' I said.

'Surely one of the crew will have been before.' She really was trying to help. 'Couldn't you ask them?'

I chuckled. 'Don't worry about it, honey. I'll just follow the signposts.'

Now she knew that she was out of her depth. I really must know what I was doing.

'Well, I wish you luck. Keep safe and try to do two quick trips. You'd better ring me after the last one! Now I know the name of the ship I'll watch for it in arrivals in the *Hull Daily Mail*.'

'There's no danger of me not ringing this time. I'm sorry I won't have time to see you this weekend.' I blew her a little kiss over the phone and left it at that.

The *St Keverne* was moored up on the south side of the dock, bow to the quay in the middle of a line of overlapping ships, their sterns held off by the bow of the adjoining vessel. Access to the ship was by a ten-foot step-ladder resting on the fore-deck rail. I paid off the taxi, carried my case up the ladder, swung it up and balanced it on top of the rail. A deck-hand lingering on the fore-deck stepped forward, took it from me and stood it down. Not because I was the skipper, but because I was a shipmate.

'Do you know where the watchman is?' I asked him, picking up my case.

'Aft side, I believe, Skipper.'

'Go and ask him if he's got my keys will you? I'm going up to my berth.'

He started aft ahead of me and spied a shipmate further aft still. 'Hey, tell the watchman the Old Man's aboard. He wants his keys up at his cabin.' The other man acknowledged him and disappeared.

Old man! I thought. At twenty-six. Time is passing quickly.

I climbed the steps cut into the accommodation side in the middle of the ship, a big improvement on the sheer metal ladder of older vessels. Reaching the first of the verandas (the one above led to the bridge), I opened the door to the flat that was home to the skipper and the wireless operator, plus the bond locker. The bulkheads were lined with polished, mahogany-stained wood, and the passageway was covered with patterned coconut matting. Passing the small operator's berth, I arrived at the door of the master's cabin, just in time to see the old watchman appear at the top of the internal stairway, hurrying to put the key in the Yale lock.

I stepped into a fully carpeted, lounge-type reception room with polished built-in cabinets and cupboards. Below two round port-holes, cushioned seat lockers surrounded the front of the cabin, and a small bedroom led off to the left. All in all, it was a palace compared with the other accommodation on the ship.

'Your bond's all aboard and under seal, Skipper,' the grinning watchman told me unnecessarily. I thanked him, putting my hand in my back pocket and handing him a ten-shilling note. That would equal about a third of his wages for the two and a half days he'd just spent aboard, small fry compared to the money he would have earned in his earlier years as a deck-hand or engineer. He thanked me and left. The table in the middle of the room was covered with a velvet cloth and littered with notices to the master from the company and the various Merchant Marine and insurance offices. I glanced through them all to check they contained nothing needing my attention before we sailed, then I made my way to the bridge.

The radio operator was already testing the radar, which would run now till the end of the trip. A chart of the river lay on the chart-room table, left there by the previous skipper. Everything seemed to be in order. I dropped the bridge front window and looked out at the busy dock. A number of ships were preparing to leave. Benny, the ship's runner, was weaving his way through the dock-side jumble on his bike. Jack Gibby had retired, and Benny was now in charge of the crew signings. No doubt he was coming to let me know all was correct. He'd be impatient for me to sail before anything went wrong. Once we were on our way, his job became easier – for the time being at least.

Then my heart jumped as a familiar figure in a purple jacket and high heels came clipping across the swing- bridge. She was dressed like Janet, but people were constantly pushing past her on the crossing and I couldn't quite see clearly enough. My heart was racing. Janet wouldn't know it was unlucky for women to see fishermen off on the dock. I lifted the ship's binoculars to my eyes and my pulse subsided. Thank goodness, it wasn't my current girlfriend, just an office girl in similar clothes. I would have to cast all girls out of my mind now for the next three weeks.

'You're cleared for leaving,' said Benny. 'And everyone's present and correct.'

I walked across to the engine-room telegraph and rang stand by, audible all round the accommodation as well as down in the engine room. The engineers replied, and men began to amble along the decks to their positions as Benny shook my hand and left the bridge.

Just then, two ships further down the dock gave two long blasts and two short on their whistles, calling for a tug to pull them off the berth and into the lock. The helmsman was already in position and I decided to move now on my own. 'Put the wheel hard to starboard,' I told him. 'Cast everything off aft. Hold on to the fore spring rope only.' Ringing slow ahead for two or three turns of the propeller then stop with the wheel to starboard kicked the stern away from the vessel inside very nicely. Then two or three turns astern then stop allowed the ship to drift slowly backwards into the dock.

I knew quite a number of eyes would be on me, aware that it was my first trip as skipper. Some would be watching my every move to see if I made any mistakes – not least my father and the gaffer from his office. Others would just be interested in seeing a ship manoeuvre in such a tight space.

Wheel hard a-port and another kick ahead then stop and she swung nicely in her own length to line up with the dock entrance. Slow ahead and we moved slowly away, the first ship to leave. As we passed through the lock, Benny was on one side as usual and his assistant Billy on the other.

The long blast on the whistle as we moved out into the Humber was exhilarating. This was a unique experience. I was in charge of a vessel costing over a million pounds and could take it almost anywhere I liked so long as I caught a saleable trip of fish. It was special indeed.

The comparatively short three-day run up to Iceland was uneventful. The weather was fine, as you would expect in late summer, and everything went as normal. The bridge was cleaned every morning before I appeared, the brass shining brightly. The mate and bosun preparing the trawl approached me separately to check what specifications I required. Otherwise the business of making ready for fishing moved ahead steadily with few interruptions from me.

Helped by the wireless operator, my job was to locate the fish. Trawler skippers didn't bandy information about when they met with success. If they did, they'd be swamped with vessels in no time, and you couldn't afford to help the opposition too much. As a new skipper I had no contacts apart from my counterparts in our company, who reported to the office each day at a scheduled time. However, when skippers were chatting to friends they often spoke about places where they'd drawn a blank. You just had to keep your ear to the ground.

My officers made a few subtle probes as they tried to find out where I might start fishing, but I kept my own counsel. I had it in my mind to carry on for an extra day's steaming round to the North Cape. It was a favourite area of mine and the one I knew best. But I would have been flexible enough to alter my plans had we received any indications of fish along the way. I resisted the urge to try out other spots I knew because I was wary of wasting time. Fishing was always poor at this time of year and, if they could, most top skippers stopped for their holidays. That's why I was in a ship like the *Keverne*.

I went straight to the North Cape Bank, real name Stranda Flak, and we shot our gear along the east edge in a depth of 105 to 110 fathoms. I towed in towards the land, following the so-called Fairy River. But, before we could get into it properly, I found we were approaching the Icelanders new limit-line. Scanning the mountains ahead of us through the binoculars, I noticed a peak with a little corner sticking out half-way down. The peak resembled the edge of a sloping roof and it reminded me of a tow my father used to talk about. He said it looked like you were opening and shutting the attic window. *This* must be the mountain involved. Perhaps it looked like an attic window from further in, but the extension of the limit-line now denied us this view.

The tow produced a bag of fifty baskets. It was mostly cod but it also included a lot of small red fish. That was no good to us, so I moved further out along the edge and into deeper water. This was much more worthwhile, producing two bags of cod with only a few red fish. When the crew were gutting, however, I noticed something significant. The fish had no substantial food in their pokes and were obviously feeding on anything they could find. They clearly weren't going to last, and indeed they were gone by the end of the day.

Avoiding the bad ground, I searched all over Stranda Flak but I couldn't find enough fish to satisfy us. Time then to steam to the next bank, Skaga Flak (or Skaggi to us fishermen). Again I knew the location of the bad ground, and there were some wonderful haddock to be had there when the time was right, but this wasn't it. A great pity, the fish we did catch were like bars of silver. That was the point about the Icelandic grounds. In season they were prolific and the quality was the best you could find. But the bottom was rough and uneven, with many crevices and ravines. That made many of them difficult to work and gave most crews a lot of mending to do.

This wasn't the case with the *Keverne*, but we weren't catching enough either, so inevitably I finished up in the bad ground chasing the elusive fish. In the end I did all right for the time of year, returning with an acceptable trip, not marvellous but acceptable. We landed a total of 1580 ten-stone kits and realised £5866 – not a bad return on a poor market. The gaffer didn't seem too disappointed. It more or less compared with the other ships landing that day. We decided that I'd go to Bear Island for my next trip. Then he sent me off for my two-day break.

The extra settling due to me as skipper was very acceptable. Most of it would go in the bank. But what could I do with a pocketful to spend? Especially as Janet was away in London. None of my other close friends were around. I hadn't heard from Terry for a while – like me, he had been sailing as mate and must have been ready to go skipper – and my other fishing pals from schooldays were always at sea. Meanwhile Geoff, the shore-based pal I'd always relied upon, had got himself a good job in London. It made me long even more for Janet.

Anyway, I still had ship's business to occupy me, first of all ordering my duty-free. I had two or three stores to choose from but made my way to the one used by most skippers in my firm. When I entered the reception room of the large store just off the dock, a double surprise awaited me. The large, comfy sofa on one side of the room was occupied by Leif Larsen and family, including wife Jean and daughter Christina. Seeing Lugs again was something of a shock. I had managed to avoid him since those traumatic days when I sailed with him as a decky before I went to hospital. He had treated me appallingly, and it still rankled.

But, of course, I had met up with the delightful Christina on a couple of occasions since then. And who should be sitting opposite them but my buddy Eddie Woolford. All had a drink in front of them, passing the time of day while they ordered their stores. Apparently Eddie was just about to embark on his first trip as skipper, while Larsen was managing to stay in the *St Britwin*, one of the firm's better ships. Still, the *Britwin* wasn't as big as the *Keverne*, and the old Dane must have found it irritating to see me in command. I could expect no favours from him, I knew.

Christina, however, was delighted to see me. The store manager, Stan Warner, served me with a gin and tonic, and Chris quickly moved to sit alongside me on the double settee. Eddie was helping to organise a little birthday party and buffet for a college pal of ours, and Christina joined in our conversation enthusiastically. A few minutes later Stan handed some papers to Larsen, concluding their business. 'Time we got going,' he said, in his strong Danish accent. 'Finish your drink if you want a lift home, Christina.'

'I want to stay chatting to Bob and Eddie for a bit longer,' she replied. 'Have you got your car with you, Bob?' she asked, turning to me. 'Could you give me a lift home?'

'Of course,' I replied. No reason why not. So that was agreed, and Lugs and his wife went on their way.

Eddie and I carried on chatting while we ordered our stores. 'Why don't you come and join us at the party this afternoon?' he asked. 'Chris could come along too.'

'I'd love to', said Christina, a twinkle in her eye. 'But I've got to get back to Leeds and I'll end up missing my train. Would you mind driving me back, Bob?'

Did I have a choice? What could I do but say yes?

We agreed to meet up with Eddie at the St Andrew's Club, a venue I didn't often frequent. In fact, I hadn't been there since my last trip as bosun with Dusty Rhodes, when he didn't let on that I was going mate.

I enjoyed meeting up with old friends again, and it was good to have a laugh about our days at the Nautical School. Until, that is, someone started mentioning the name of Miss Webb. Time to leave before Christina heard too much. 'Come on, Chris,' I said. 'We'd better get moving if we're to get back to Leeds before tea.'

We collected Chris's things from home and set off for Leeds. To be frank, I was feeling a bit tense after meeting up with Lugs Larsen again. I knew I had to deliver a good trip next time to earn another chance, and it wouldn't be easy to compete against the likes of Lugs. But Chrissie helped me keep my mind off such matters. What a lovely girl, I thought, as she sat alongside me in the car. Slim, blonde *and* curvaceous. Her eyes still sparkled every time she smiled at me and she hung on to my arm when the roads were straight.

'Isn't it time you thought about getting married now you're a skipper?' she remarked cheekily.

'It is time I moved away from home,' I replied. 'But it might not be easy to find a girl who'd put up with a guy who spends so much time at sea.'

'No problem there,' she giggled. 'I'm used to the man of the house being at sea.'

Lugs Larsen for a father-in-law. What a dreadful idea! Now that would cause problems for a start – for both of us. 'I'm afraid you're not the type who'd wait at home till I got back,' I ventured.

Clinging to my arm, Chris started stroking the inside of my thigh with her other hand. 'Well, not stay at home exactly. You've got to get out and circulate. But I would stay true to you.'

'It wouldn't work out, Chris. You've got your own career in Leeds.'

'I could always put in for a transfer.'

'But that would interfere with your studies,' I insisted. 'Anyway let's leave it for now.'

We soon reached the Leeds Ring Road. 'We're back much earlier than I thought,' said Chris. 'And I don't want to get in too soon. Can I show you a little hollow I know? You can sometimes see deer and rabbits skipping about there and feeding together.'

'Are you kidding me?' I grinned at her. 'There's no chance of that happening in the next half hour or so.'

'There is, really. You just turn off into this field further up on the right.'

We followed a track which led up a slope and right into a copse of trees before petering out on a grassy knoll. I manoeuvred the car round until it was facing the grassy dell Chris had described, and then we sat and waited. The odd glimpse of afternoon sun shining through the trees reflected off the greens and browns of the leaves and branches. It made them look quite magical, if you exercised a little imagination.

'Put a little music on, Rob,' Chris murmured, snuggling up to me. 'We won't disturb anything if you keep it low.' She had undone the top two buttons of her dress, exposing firm, rounded breasts, nicely pushed up by her bra. 'Do you remember when we were young and made love in that open field? It was so exciting.' Draping her arm across my chest, she massaged my neck and tickled the lobe of my right ear, at the same time covering my face with gentle kisses. Her sensual movements and the sound of her breathing were definitely having an effect.

Suddenly we sensed movement, although not of the kind we were expecting. Another car was coming up the track. I could see it through the trees. It was an ordinary saloon like mine, clean and polished. I switched on my lights and flashed the intruders through the loose foliage. Success! They stopped in their tracks and turned round. 'Some other nature-lovers,' I joked as we watched them depart. Giggling, Chris slid down in her seat with her arms round my neck, pulling me with her.

As I flopped on top of her, my nose finished up between those two fleshy mounds. Chris was wearing a strapless bra! When could she have put that on? Probably when she collected her things, I thought. The tempting little sex siren must have planned it all from the start. She was better at this than me. I pushed the dress off her shoulder, pulled down her bra and began to nibble at the firm flesh beneath, seeking to be as inventive as possible with my lips and my tongue. Meanwhile Chris began to moan and gasp and writhe beneath me, arching her back and spreading her legs. I was quite overwhelmed by the desire shown by this coquette. I needed satisfaction but just as much I needed to satisfy her. Our union again produced a feeling of warmth and tingling, relief and gratitude mingling with a certain moistness below.

As we came up for air, all the recent tension and worry drained from my body. 'Look,' said Chris suddenly. A young deer was drinking from the pool of water while rabbits scampered around behind it. 'See, that's what *I* came up here for.'

'Me too,' I drawled disbelievingly. 'Now we're both satisfied.'

Chris put on a bit of a show when we got back to her place. A couple of her colleagues were talking in the entrance so just to impress them she gave me a great big hug and a smoochy kiss. I drove away certain that she'd be telling them both that I was a ship's captain.

CHAPTER 13

THE GLASS SOU'WESTER

The following day I was once again back on the Humber, navigating my ship downriver without a pilot, a privilege allowed to trawler skippers. We were heading for Bear Island, more than 500 miles inside the Arctic Circle and much further away than Iceland, and it would take us over five days to get there. It was still only early autumn and the weather was OK during our first two days running NNE across the North Sea. The wind was in the NW, about Force Four, with the waves running between four and six feet high. The odd breaker slapped the rail hard enough to cast a light spray across the deck, but the men putting the gear in place could work with little discomfort.

I had been surprised, and not a little disconcerted, to discover that one of the changes to my crew was my old school pal Charlie. We had sailed together as decky learners and young deckies. But, much to Charlie's disgust, we hadn't seen each other since I stopped to study for my bosun's ticket and he moved on to another company. The first time we met on deck, we acknowledged each other with a grin and a nod. However, I'd since said little when he had the wheel, preferring to busy myself with navigating the ship.

Two days out, we made our first contact with Norway when we passed Stadlandet Corner, keeping a look-out for the Svinøy Lighthouse. Then we enjoyed another good day's sailing as far as the Arctic Circle. But after that the weather began to deteriorate. The wind veered to the north, increasing to Force Seven or Eight, while the seas built up to fifteen to twenty feet and came rushing at us at speed, eventually stopping most of the work. All we could do was press our foreheads against the bridge windows and watch as the bows of the ship slammed into one wall of water after another. Each one shook the ship from end to end, almost enough to work the rivets loose, as the fo'c'sle head chopped the tops off each wave and threw tens of tonnes of water at the bridge front.

We had all seen this a hundred times before, and I had always accepted it as inevitable. But as skipper I felt responsible, since I was the only one who could take avoiding action – and the crew knew it. I *could* have eased the ship in. But Lugs Larsen had sailed the day before me and I couldn't afford to let him get too big a start, especially when the chances were that he'd missed this weather. Anyway, most other skippers would keep going too. We just had to tough it out. But I was aware of the looks that Charlie and the others kept giving me.

It was uncomfortable and depressing for us all. As I watched another wave-top exploding from the stem, throwing a torrent of angry white water across the deck and at the bridge windows, my mind flashed back just five days earlier to a rather different scene and the lovely soft colours of a country dell. Then an extra thump bashed my nose against the bridge windows and brought me quickly back to down to earth.

Twelve hours later, the weather had begun to moderate and we made better progress up to the extensive fishing grounds around Bear Island. By the following day, the sea-bed had at last started to shoal out into fishable waters and a large group of ships was emerging on the radar. So many vessels packed so close together could indicate only one thing – a fish shop, as the skippers termed it, a large shoal of fish.

We soon had the boys out, and before long I was heading straight into the pack and shooting my trawl. The ships were working in and around a depth of 150 fathoms and we had to stream three times that amount astern. So each vessel was towing more than half a mile of wire, something to bear in mind when you were pushing past and crossing other ships. It was going to be a good examination of my concentration and nerve, that was for sure.

As it turned out, I was tested immediately. Two vessels were crossing close ahead of me, one from either bow. I made sure I kept straight till they were clear, but beyond them, and heading directly towards me on the stem, another two foreign ships were tight side by side, trying to push each other out of the best water. I had no chance to get across either of them. All I could do was hold my course, heading straight for them.

The vessels reluctantly separated just enough for me to squeeze through. But could we clear our gear given the spread between the otter-boards? I had visions of all three of us tangling our nets, and on my first tow too! It would cause lots of damage and take hours to sort out. Somehow we managed to keep clear – I don't know how, but the sea-bed is a curious place with its mounds and crevices – and I was able to plough on further into the mêlée. I was up and down on the bridge, keeping an eye on the echo-sounder, all the while watching from one side and then the other as ships aimed to pass close astern of me. I had to stay in the best fishing waters if I could.

Two hours later the net was on its way to the surface. The bag shot up crammed with fish, almost leaping from the water. The inflated stomachs of the fish made the belly of the trawl lay out on the surface, and I could see we had a good three bags, around 160 to 170 baskets. The haul had been well worth the effort. But we had to do it again and again if we could. Voices constantly blasted from the radio speakers on the bridge – some ships trying to keep clear of each other, others reporting on the results of each haul – all of it helping me to keep tabs on the movement of the main shoal. Some ships were catching far more than us, and I was trying, with difficulty, to pick out the most successful among the clutter to identify where to go next.

I couldn't leave the bridge. Only the skipper can take the risks sometimes necessary in a situation like this, and things remained unchanged for the next two or three days, giving me no chance to grab any sleep. Eventually, unsettled by the constant disturbance, the shoal began to disperse, and with it the pack as individual vessels departed to search for the odd clumps of fish now settling here and there.

The group contained two more of our firm's ships and I spoke to them both. One of the skippers was Lugs Larsen. Lugs seemed to be doing a bit better than me – or so he said, anyway. I knew skippers indulged in a lot of deceit and misinformation as they tried to outwit each other, and it all put more strain on me. I managed the odd hour or two of sleep over the next couple of days, but that was all. The mate could only do the tow I had given him, and every time I returned to the bridge it seemed as if someone else had found a new clump of fish and we were once again in the wrong place.

The days were passing quickly. Soon it would be time to set off home. We had been doing OK but I still had the feeling that others were doing better. I decided to take the plunge and steam in towards Bear Island as far as the 100-fathom line to work an area called the South-East Gullies and Finger Banks. We took the gear aboard and I steamed north till we reached a point just short of the 100-fathom line. Then I shot in 105 fathoms and towed towards one of the fingers. We had steamed about forty miles, but I could still hear the ships talking faintly in the distance on the VHF. It sounded like a couple of boats might have caught up with the fish again, each having hauled with eighty baskets.

Then came another haul even further away. I couldn't hear properly but it was obviously causing some excitement. By the sound of it, they had definitely caught up with the fish again. Then I heard Lugs' heavily accented tones. 'It's no good trying to contact the *Keverne*. He'll be too far away by now. Anyway, he took a chance. He might as well stick with it.'

My heart sank. I'd steamed away from the fish. Had I been too hasty? I wondered. Should I have shown a bit more patience? Was this something I still had to learn? I looked around at the empty grey sea. I was hoping to find a good haul of fish, immediately and on my own. There are thousands of square miles of sea without any fish out there. It usually takes time to catch up with them and I had only a couple of days at most.

With no fish on the deck, the bosun – whose watch it was – was helping me on the bridge when I decided to shoot the gear. Raising one eyebrow, he looked at me askance. But I had no time to say anything in my defence before some bright flashes suddenly appeared on the fish loupe. I hadn't been using the loupe earlier but I had switched it on when we shot in this lonely place. It had a flashing strobe that picked up on fish in quantity and magnified the signal when you passed over them.

I immediately glanced over at the echo-sounder, but it was showing nothing. Our gear was just climbing up on to one of the fingers, the steep little edge showing eighty-five fathoms. 'Did you see that?' I asked my second officer. 'There *are* fish around here somewhere. I'll search around these little banks. You keep watching the fish loupe.'

'Aye aye, Skipper,' he replied. 'What am I looking for?'

I explained how the loupe worked, then carried on pulling the ship around from one depth to another, climbing on and off the Finger Bank and plotting on the chart. What showed as an occasional flash on the loupe appeared as nothing special on the echo-sounder – just a slight thickening of the line marking the sea-bed. An hour and a half later I was beginning to lose heart again. Impatiently, I decided to haul early and have a look.

A wry smile on his face, the bosun left the bridge to help to bring up the trawl. Meanwhile I continued manoeuvring the ship till the gear was nearly at the surface, then I stopped her and watched the trawl come up. The mouth of the trawl bobbed up close to the side. But like everyone else I was staring at the water thirty or forty yards away, looking for the patch of light-green, effervescent water that always precedes any bag of fish.

The sparks came out of the wireless room. 'It's company sched time,' he said. 'What shall I tell 'em?'

'Say we're searching the South-East Gullies.'

I continued to stare at the water, my excitement mounting as a light green patch came zooming up from the depths and a round bag hit the surface and rolled over. Whoopee! It looked too much for one bag, probably ninety to a hundred baskets. All for just one ninety-minute tow.

Thank you, Lord. There must be plenty of fish around here. All I had to do now was search it out and quickly. I needed to get a marker buoy down straight away.

I decided to concentrate our search on the point where we'd first spotted the fish, where the bottom edge of the finger meets the flat. That's where the current hits, stirring up the minerals from the sea-bed. I also decided to tow up the gully, between the fingers, where the fish sought respite from the constant flow of water. Over the next twelve hours we doubled or tripled our hauls. The deck was loaded because the crew just couldn't keep it clear.

At sched time the next day I was able to report a 600-kit day – the equivalent of two good days' work in one. Then I listened in to try and catch the response. All I could hear was Lugs. He was calling Freddie Mason, our other skipper. 'Hey, have you seen what the *Keverne* has put on the sched. If it's right, we better get over there.'

Marvellous! With all those ships around him listening in, Lugs had only gone and given the game away. While mentioning no figures, he'd said enough for my competitors to realise that I was doing better than they were, especially those that were missing the big hauls. Within another twelve hours I wouldn't be able to move. It would be no problem for Lugs. After all, he was leaving the following day. But I reckon he was worried about me. He wouldn't want this upstart catching more than him – and sending a massive influx of ships in my direction was one way of handicapping me.

Still, I was confident. By the time I was forced off the fish, I might already have caught enough to leave a day earlier than planned. We would just have to wait and see.

Fred knew exactly where I was, and he was the first to arrive. 'How are you working,' he asked, spotting the marker buoy. Then he shot away and left the mate to do the tow while he went to bed. He must have been spending long hours on the bridge working among all those ships. But then so had I. And I'd been up searching for the best fishing ever since we steamed here. It was days since my last decent nap. My eyes were red raw and my shoulders stiff with tension. I had intended to grab a couple of hours' sleep while the boys cleared some of the fish, but with other vessels appearing on the horizon I decided to get a couple of hauls in while I still had room to manoeuvre.

Every ship that turned up headed straight towards me, since it was the *St Keverne* that was supposed to be on the fish, and my hauls got progressively smaller as they crowded me out. I was keeping a beady eye on Lugs Larsen. He was now working towards the southerly edge of the group, no doubt hoping to get away before anyone noticed, and I decided to work in the same direction. On our next tow I spotted Lugs through the glasses. He had his gear aboard and was rapidly disappearing over the horizon, clearly after getting the best position on the market. I couldn't afford to allow him too much of a start, though the *Keverne* was marginally faster than his ship. The difference between us was less than a quarter of a knot, but I reckoned that should be enough to catch him over five days.

'Get the gear aboard and stow it,' I told the lads when we hauled. That brought a bit of a cheer. Now they were certain we were going home. But what could I do about my buoy? If I steamed back to collect it from the middle of the pack, and then wasted even more time picking it up with its wire and anchor, I would never catch Lugs. But the trouble was these big buoys were expensive. Fortunately, I had an idea which might kill two birds with one stone.

I called up Freddie Mason, knowing that Lugs wasn't yet out of radio distance and would surely be listening in. 'Fred,' I said. 'Do you want me to leave my buoy down for you when we haul, and charge it to you when I get home?'

'Yes, please,' said Fred, leaving Lugs in the mistaken belief that I still had to haul and get my gear aboard, when in fact I was already steaming south.

I set my course on SSW, heading straight for the UK. Lugs would probably be taking a different route, steaming south towards Norway and then along the coast. All was right with the world. We had a good trip in, the third hand was on the wheel, and I was looking forward to lying down in the chart-room for a while until we'd cleared the fish and the watches started. And then it started to snow, quickly impairing visibility. Just my luck, I was going to need an extra look-out.

With snow beginning to stick to the bridge windows, I stuck my head out to see what was happening. Though still very tired, I felt good and decided to give the lads an hour clearing fish before I called for help. Down on the fore-deck, my old buddy Charlie was scampering off to the drying-room to change his cap for a sou'wester. I couldn't resist a bit of a dig. 'What sort of a sailor are you?' I asked him. 'Changing into a sou'wester for a little bit of snow?

'It's OK for you,' he shouted back. 'You've got that big glass sou'wester up there.' That caused a bit of a laugh. True, it did shield me from the weather. But I'd spent a long time on that bridge, and the cover it provided did nothing to help my swollen ankles.

We entered the Humber and checked in at the Killingholme anchorage so far ahead of Lugs Larsen that the gaffers were able to redirect us to catch the tide at Grimsby – the market there must have been short of fish. The following day we landed the equivalent of 2800 kits, or 3500 boxes in Grimsby, realising a total of £9300. Not a bad return at a time when the markets were poor.

We returned to Hull the same day to find I was company champion for that trip. Lugs had landed over 400 kits fewer than us and made a much smaller return, as the Hull market hadn't been as good. I knew my old adversary would be livid; he'd certainly be on the look-out for any chance to do me down in future.

With my two trips over and done I was expecting to sign off. The *Keverne* was Alf Farguson's ship, after all. And he was one of the firm's top skippers. But a surprise awaited me when I went up to see the big boss. Apparently he was the one who had backed me to start in a big ship, against the advice of my more cautious father, and he was delighted by my success. For its next trip, they wanted to send the *Keverne* to Greenland, the only place then reporting any substantial amounts of fish. Farguson, of course, refused to go there and was prepared to have another trip off. I would get another chance, though Greenland was a big challenge for any new skipper.

I was walking on air. And, having landed in Grimsby, we had an extra night in dock. I couldn't wait to ring Janet when she left work. Perhaps I could take her out for a meal. Jan was thrilled when I rang. Although unable to tell a good trip from a bad one, she knew how happy I was. She was also intrigued by the idea of going out on an evening just for a meal, but I could go one better than that. I planned to take her to the White House Hotel. Its restaurant had a little dance area, and it often had a pianist or even a quartet playing for an hour or so.

We agreed that I would go round to Jan's house in good time after work. Meantime all I had to do was order the bonded stores again and sign for them so the day was going to drag till I picked her up. I decided to go home and get some of my kit packed, but what I really needed was a bit of time on my own. I also needed to get moving on finding a place of my own.

Driving home, I spotted a corner house nearing completion on the edge of an estate still under construction only a few miles from our village. The house was a different build and better finished than the rest, and I decided to stop and investigate further. Two men were inside, working hard on the finishing touches. They were brothers who worked for themselves and obviously took pride in everything they did. The house suited me perfectly: three bedrooms, through lounge with French windows, big kitchen and a large corner garden with separate garage. It wasn't yet up for sale but they were able to give me a price. I reckoned I could afford it and decided to take matters further.

Janet took me by surprise when I knocked on her door that evening. 'Why don't you come in while I finish getting ready?' she said. As far as I could see she looked perfect already. Perhaps her parents wanted an excuse to look me over. I felt pretty confident. After all I was driving my own car and was smartly dressed in my brand-new, camel-hair raglan overcoat.

'You're very tall,' said her mother. 'Much taller than I expected.'

Her dad too was all smiles. 'You don't look at all like a fisherman,' he commented. I replied neutrally, resisting the temptation to ask what he thought a fisherman *should* look like. All in all, we left them in a happy and relaxed frame of mind.

Although the White House was not a regular venue for me, I'd been a couple of times with the family and knew what to expect. It was a bit more up-market than most of the other restaurants around Hull, but I had a table booked and walked in with confidence. It certainly impressed Janet with its style and intimacy, even if it was only half full this early in the evening. Despite the extensive menu, I stuck with steak, while Janet chose lobster thermidor, and even though I'm not a wine drinker I thought it appropriate to order a couple of glasses.

I was hoping Jan would find the place romantic and her eyes glowed as she took in the plush décor and special service. As the night wore on, the subdued lighting and a few sips of wine also had their effect, and she was soon gazing softly into my eyes, especially when the little quartet started playing. We were on the coffee and liqueurs when Janet finally took my hand and asked for a dance. There was only one other couple on the floor as Jan snuggled into me rather sleepily. The feel of her body through her thin dress was so exciting because this was a kitten who *wanted* to be close. We had a couple of dances that night, our smouldering gazes and little touches around the face and neck making plain our strong feelings for each other.

When the band stopped for a break, I thought it a good moment to leave, especially if we wanted to spend some intimate time together. Close to Janet's home, I pulled off on to some spare ground alongside a railway embankment. I parked the car among some bushes and looked out from the shadows at the quiet urban streets. Jan was worried for me. We'd been discussing my next trip to Greenland, and what it would be like to take a ship across the Atlantic into ice-infested waters. But now she snuggled close. 'Thanks for a wonderful night,' she said, kissing me full on the lips. 'I wish you didn't have to go away again so soon.'

She was so lovely and loving. Dizzy with desire, I caressed her hair and neck while we exchanged long, silky kisses. Pretty soon my excitement was growing as I let my hand slide down to her smooth, pert breast. Jan was leaning her head back and moaning gently between our kisses. Then suddenly her body went taut and she began to tremble slightly.

Although no less filled with desire, Jan obviously wasn't happy with what we were doing and was only allowing it to please me. I took my hand away and whispered an apology. Wrapping my arms tight around her, I hugged her close. We clung together, rocking a little to the low music issuing from the car radio. The warmth and the vibes flowing from Jan's body into mine had a hypnotic effect. I was glowing with pleasure and satisfaction in the sure knowledge that she was getting as much out of our encounter as me.

Mesmerised by the feel and scent of Jan's hair, I didn't want the evening to end. But the radio announcer reminded us of the time and I didn't want to spoil things with her parents. 'Come on, it's getting late,' I said. 'If you've work in the morning I'd better get you back. Your parents won't think much of me otherwise.' I tried to move away but Janet had her head stuck to my chest like a limpet. I eased her off, then with a little kiss on her forehead I turned to start the engine.

The curtain was twitching again when I pulled up outside Jan's house. A quick kiss to end the evening, then she turned to go. 'Don't forget we sail tomorrow night,' I said. 'I'll pop round and see you after work. I could meet you there.'

'Oh no, Rob,' she moaned. ' You can't. I've got an interview for a new job. I won't be able to see you before you go.'

'Oh dear,' I sighed. 'That's the rub with this job, I'm afraid. I'll be thinking of you, though. Bye, darling.' I leaned forward and kissed her again.

'Do be careful out there,' she said, and disappeared into the house.

The next day was a busy one, dealing with the building society and the solicitors. Then it was goodbye to Mum and the family, and all aboard to sail at seven p.m.

I hated sailing at that time of day because the boozy boys had always drunk too much and were a nuisance on the first day. Fortunately, there were usually enough sensible men to cover for them, but there had been some changes this trip. Two or three, the bosun included, had stopped at home for a break. They could afford it after our previous trip. Appropriately enough, the new bosun was called Fish, Joe Fish. He was new to the company, and neither the mate nor I knew him, but he was just sober enough to organise the clean-up of the deck when we cleared the port.

Insurance rules demanded that the mate, Alan Bradshaw, remained on the bridge with me until we cleared the river. A shipmate who had followed me through the ranks in different ships over the years, Alan knew my quirks, and my quick temper.

Once beyond the Humber I set a heading to clear Flamborough Head. Then we would alter course for Duncansby Head at the entrance to the Pentland Firth. I prepared for another six days' steaming before we reached the fishing grounds, plenty of time to fix the gear to my way of working. The mate took over the watch, but I spent some time in the wireless room with the sparks, Kenny Ward. Kenny had been an operator in the firm since I was just a decky, and if there was any information out there he would find it. He picked up titbits from ships returning home from the White Sea and Iceland, but we heard nothing of any ships coming back from Greenland.

Since it was dark, I remained on and around the bridge until we had passed Flamborough and the bosun had taken over. Joe seemed all right after a bit of a nap and I left him to it. The next morning was fine and the bridge looked to have been cleaned well enough, although I wouldn't have tolerated the small residue of Brasso visible in the creases of the brass telegraph had it not been our first twelve hours away. The mate had the daymen on the deck fixing a trawl together to put alongside ready for shooting. From the speed they were working some still had a hangover, but that was nothing unusual. They would pull round as the day progressed.

I spent the morning in my berth studying some Greenland charts, trying to decide where to begin fishing. The young boss had instructed me to bypass the southerly grounds. Apparently he'd received information indicating that it would be a waste of time. I could understand why he wouldn't want me following Rowan Berkeley's example and going close in around the Cape area. But I'd seen some great fishing at this time of year just around the corner in Julianehaab Bay, and he was asking me to miss out on that too. We'd have to see what information we could pick up on the way across.

Lugs Larsen was also heading in the same direction. He was two days ahead of us and once he started fishing would have to report his whereabouts on the company schedule.

At noon the bosun took over the deck and the men continued working on the net. I relaxed by reading up on some ice manuals for a while, then I went over to the wireless room to listen to the BBC News and see what Ken had found out. Crossing the bridge, I noticed the deck was empty. 'Where is everyone?' I asked the wheelman. He looked a bit edgy, but I thought he was concentrating on maintaining his course while I was watching him.

'The lads have all gone for a drink,' he replied.

'What, as early as this?'

Still, I knew they wouldn't have gone down without the bosun's permission.

I continued into the wireless room and listened to the news with the sparks. Then Ken called up Wick radio to see if they had any traffic for us, picking up a lovey-dovey telegraph for one of the crew. Meanwhile I walked back to the bridge to see how things stood. To my surprise there was still no one out on deck. I decided not to quiz the wheelman again. He wouldn't know what was going on, though he was staring intently at the compass with the air of a man who didn't want to get involved.

I continued over to the companion-way and the steps that led down, first to my flat and then to the officers' cabins below. The sound of voices and laughter came drifting faintly up towards me. I went down one flight of steps and stopped at the top of the next, just outside my cabin door. From here, I could recognise the voices of the bosun and some of the new deckies. It sounded like a bit too much merriment. And they shouldn't have been in there anyway.

At the bottom of the second flight of stairs, the door to the little vestibule of the officers' quarters was slightly ajar, giving a clear view through to the bosun's berth, and the shoulder of a decky lounging, beer in hand, within. It looked like there was a right little party going on. I stepped forward quickly. Three deckies and two learners were squatting around the little cabin, drink in hand. Meanwhile the bosun was sitting on the edge of his bunk, and in the middle of the floor was a half-full hessian sack. I picked it up and looked in, amazed to see so many bottles of beer, plus a couple of spirits. How on earth could so much booze still be available this far into the trip?

I turned to the bosun. 'What are you larking at?' I asked him. 'Why aren't these men working on deck? You know it's illegal to bring booze on board.' (True enough, although few crewmen ever paid much attention to the rule.) 'Get these men out on deck now and I'll take charge of this.'

Leaning forward, I grabbed the neck of the sack, quickly lifted it out of the berth and hauled it up the stairs. Behind me, I could hear the men starting to protest. 'He can't do that. It's yours. I'll go and get it back.'

Opening the door to my berth, I put the sack in sharp, then turned back to block the way. The first of the irate deckies had appeared on the stairs, another following close behind. I wasn't going to allow them up to start an argument. 'You'll only make things worse coming up here,' I said. 'Get back to work. You should have been out there twenty minutes ago.'

The decky continued on up. 'We just want a word, Skipper. That's all. You can't take things off people like that.'

I gave him a final warning: 'Get out on deck now and do the job you're paid for.'

Still he kept on coming. When the time was right, I placed my foot on top of his head and thrust down hard. The decky lost his grip and tumbled to the bottom, banging his head on the bulkhead in the process. He wouldn't have felt much, but he must have been dazed because he stopped complaining for a moment. His mate stepped over him and started up too, only to meet the same fate.

Then the bosun's hand appeared. 'Come on, lads,' he said, starting to drag them away. 'You'll only make things worse for me. We've had a break. Better get back to the job now.' They started chuntering again, but the rest had seen enough and were already moving away.

I remained at the top of the stairs for a few minutes longer, reflecting on events. It reminded me of 'The Sea Witch', a film I'd seen some years before, when Edward G Robinson, as captain of a sailing vessel, kicked his crew down the fo'c'sle ladder to quell a mutiny. Perhaps not quite so dramatic but certainly in the same vein.

When I returned to the bridge, the men had taken up their braiding needles once again and were working with bad grace. They cast sullen glances in my direction, only to see me leaning on the window scowling back down at them. Only twenty-six years old maybe, but now they knew I was a skipper who insisted on good discipline.

Everyone's mood improved as we made our voyage across the Atlantic in fine, mild weather. Eventually we could see the tops of the mountains leading down to Cape Farewell, but along the shoreline they just disappeared in a long bank of fog. The temperature dropped sharply as we approached, and we soon found out why. The bank was hovering above field ice which stretched away probably as far as the land itself, still twelve miles distant.

I was shaping to pass Cape Farewell, but I couldn't pick my way through the ice in this fog. I would have to sail south and follow the edge instead, and this could cost us a lot of time. The ice might stretch up to thirty miles south before the current forced it west, while track the edge too closely and you risked being led into a big bay of ice and finding yourself forced to curl round and follow it all the way out again. Experience really came into play here.

The fog proved a real curse. First because it was so widespread, and then, once we'd rounded the ice and begun working up the west side of Greenland, because it hid any other ships scattered among the inside banks and so indicating fish in the area. My instructions had been to bypass all these southern banks. But we were still almost 400 miles from the great banks up north and we'd already lost time skirting the ice. Besides, owners shouldn't try to run a trip from behind an office desk. To them, however, I was still a novice.

All this time we had heard nothing from Lugs Larsen, not even on the company sched. The office should have picked him up about that; he was obviously sending his reports in direct.

Soon we were crossing Julianehaab Bay, where I would have preferred to begin my search. I knew the grounds well, having fished here with several skippers, and it was a large area offering plenty of scope. By now we were clear of the field ice but the fog was no less thick, and as we steamed on to Semersok Bank the radar screen was showing a number of scattered targets. Could they all be icebergs? I wondered. We had already spotted one or two.

I called Lugs on the VHF to see if he was in the area. We tried most channels but received no answer in return. Perhaps Lugs himself had gone up to the great banks? Then a large German trawler came looming out of the fog – which had now lifted to half a mile visibility – and steamed on by with some fish on his deck. He looked like he was leaving for home, but it proved there must be fish around here somewhere.

I made a quick decision, calling out the crew to shoot the trawl for a couple of exploratory tows. While we made our preparations, I searched the waters with the echo-sounder but found no indication of fish in any quantity. Still, I decided to try a couple of tows in towards the land, about thirty miles off, and find out how many of the echoes were ships. I was really searching the channels more than the waters. We hauled after two hours and brought up forty baskets of cod. Not a bad start on most other grounds but, with our time at Greenland limited, we needed much bigger pickings. I shot away again and towed further in this time, picking up some German trawlers on a couple of channels, but still no sound of an English voice.

Our second tow produced only thirty baskets of fish. It looked like I was wasting time, just what the gaffer had feared, so we got the gear aboard and started steaming north. I had decided to carry on until we reached the first of the northern banks at Frederikshaab Bay, by-passing the grounds at Cape Desolation and such as No Name Bank. At last, we escaped from the all-enveloping fog, and with the wind freshening behind us from the south we were making good progress. Then at nine p.m. we received the reports on the sched: Lugs Larsen had made a point of calling in to say that they were catching a lot of fish close in at Cape Egede.

Wasn't that just typical of Larsen? Aware from our morning report that we had left his area and were now twelve hours away to the north, he leaves it this late to make contact. He'd be in the clear if the gaffers challenged him when he got home, but it left me in a dilemma. I was nearly half way to the first of the northern banks, but I would *have* to find fish when I got there. One or two English ships were definitely up there, but I didn't know who or where they were. Lugs, on the other hand, was definitely on good fishing. It would take me at least twelve hours to steam back. But there was likely to be a bag at the end of it, providing we could keep on the fish.

We set off back, but the southerly breeze had continued to strengthen and pretty soon we were plunging into head seas which slowed our progress considerably. Then we ran into the fog again. Lugs was working just twelve miles inside our previous position in Julianehaab Bay, and I was growing ever more anxious. We had spent twelve hours steaming north, but the return journey was going to take much longer. It was all beginning to look a bit of a pantomime – but I had to show confidence in front of the crew, especially the new lads. They hadn't seen me catch fish yet.

Back in Julianehaab Bay, the swell was beginning to calm down. Then we discovered why. Growlers and ice-floes were beginning to appear: nothing better than ice for calming the waves. We were now within VHF range. I started calling Lugs and soon his voice came crackling through. 'The fog's lifting on occasion to a mile visibility,' he said. 'And I'm on the edge of the main ice-field when I get to the southern end of my tow.' The ice, of course, was moving north. Perfect! Now the ice would be pushing us off the fish.

Not me, though! Now we were back in the bay I was going to catch fish wherever it was hiding. Still, I decided to switch off the VHF speaker until the watch went on deck. They could hear too much of what was going on.

Steaming in, we passed a couple of German trawlers. Still, I wasn't going to shoot until we had identified Lugs and his companions. One was a British vessel, commanded by the flamboyant Leo Roscoe, a well-known skipper in Hull; the other, a massive French side trawler. I picked out the three ships in question at the same time as I identified fish marks on the sounder. These marks only show when there's plenty of fish around, so we shot immediately and the boys were quick to put the gear over the side.

From Lugs' report, I knew that we needed to move south from this position so I shot away in that direction, skimming between a growing number of ice-floes. Once you've shot away over 1200 feet of wire at full speed, you can't alter course to any degree, so you have to pick a strip that's clear of ice. We towed south for forty-five minutes. But the ice was becoming ever more congested and I had to start working the ship round while I could still manoeuvre sufficiently to return to the starting point.

We hauled and as the doors came up I started to search for that tell-tale patch of pale green water that would betoken a big bag. Sure enough, there it was. Pretty soon the cod-ends burst to the surface and laid out on the water, packed with inflated fish. We brought in three good bags of quality cod, or about 180 baskets – not bad for an interrupted tow. But we would need more than that to make up for the time we'd wasted. Leo Roscoe had hauled as much as 250 to 300 baskets before the ice interfered.

I had to find some gaps or lagoons in the ice. That's where the fish would be at their thickest. The ice was three feet thick and more in places, threatening the ship, but still I had to push it. Lugs, Leo and the Frenchie were each following their own leads into the ice and returning to meet up on the edge of the main pack. Meanwhile the Germans were working further off among loose growlers and bergy bits. However, there were more of them scattered around and they had better information than us.

We struggled on throughout that day, taking chances and pushing the ice about. Fortunately it is only dark for around five hours in these latitudes at this time of year. We did make two night-time tows but took fewer risks during the hours of darkness.

In the middle of the following day, the Germans informed the Frenchman that they were pulling out. Some of their ships steaming off had reported that the main ice-field, about eighty miles wide, was sweeping round outside and was about to trap us in. Germans are sensible and practical, but Englishmen are not. They are gamblers and risk-takers. 'I'm not pulling out while there's still fish to catch,' said Leo, when the Frenchman relayed the information to us. 'There's no fish out there. And we don't want to be out there wishing we were in here. Not just yet anyway.'

Lugs agreed, but then his trip was nearly complete, He had just enough to go home with, anyway. Of course, I was the freshman, there to be advised by my more experienced colleagues, so we carried on while there was still daylight. Things were getting ever more difficult. The ice got tighter as the day wore on, and we were having to push harder against the thick floes, a very dangerous practice. Still, we were heaving good hauls of fish so the lads were kept busy gutting. Making fun of the strange shapes passing by, they were happy enough. And they had confidence in me. But eventually it became difficult to find space to bring the trawl to the surface and it was obvious that we had to get out.

I was mulling on the situation when Alan joined me on the bridge. His dinner was due, and then it would be his watch below, another factor I had to take into account. Alan and I had sailed together as third hand and mate and he knew the risks I was taking. Pushing too hard against a really sharp piece of ice could puncture us. But he was pleased to see the fish-room filling up so nicely.

Next time we hauled, we took the gear on board. Leo had reported a lead just half a mile north-west of his position, heading north-westerly, and he was taking his gear on board to follow it. Lugs decided to join him. The Frenchman must have set off already because he no longer appeared on the radar, which was now giving me a wonderful picture of all the ice around, including gaps, lagoons and bergs. I was the last in line as we made our way through the ice-field. At first, I could pick out Lugs on the radar six miles ahead of us. But I was concentrating so hard on the ice around us that I lost him. Still, I knew I was on the right track because we kept spotting smudges of paint on the ice.

Lugs and I kept in touch from time to time on the VHF, both concentrating on picking our way along the narrowest of tracks. We were making reasonable progress – but then the dark closed in again. All we had to pick out the cracks between the floes were two searchlights – one fixed on the mast-head and a moveable one on the bridge – so I placed two men forr'ard on the fo'c'sle head. Bosun Fish was hard enough for this job, and his mates could interchange. Some of the floes we kept meeting were large enough to play cricket on.

Suddenly the VHF burst into life. 'I've just had a very narrow escape,' bellowed Lugs, in some agitation. 'You all need to take extra care. It's getting too risky. I'll be glad to be out of it.' The look-outs were horrified. I switched off the speaker and turned instead to the handset. How could such an experienced skipper display his alarm so openly? As Lugs told me more, his mistake became obvious. Like me, he was using the radar to pick out a track to follow, with additional men on the fore end. Spotting a clear, perfectly straight-sided channel ahead, he had made straight for it, obviously misled by a blind arc in the radar transmission caused by an obstruction.

'I could see it getting closer and closer,' Lugs continued. 'Then I was only yards away. I pushed on a bit quicker and suddenly the mate on the fo'c'sle head started screaming "Go astern before we hit this big berg".' We were all very tired, but Lugs should never have made such an error had he really understood how radar operates.

'OK, Leif,' I replied, the eyes of the men on the bridge trained upon me. 'Best of luck. We'll take it easy till daylight.' I had stopped the engines and now took hold of the bridge corner searchlight to survey the surrounding sea of ice. Everything was quiet. The fog was slowly lifting, with visibility now at about three-quarters of a mile, and the ice around the ship did not appear to be crushing us. 'OK,' I said to the mate. 'Tell the men to come down from the fore end. We'll keep an eye on her till daylight, then we'll be able to see where we're going.' Sighs of relief all round, including from the sparks, who had been listening in before disappearing back into his wireless room.

'Right, Alan,' I turned to the mate. 'This is a chance for me to get a lie-down for the first time in fifty-odd hours. Keep an eye on the sides of the ship. Make sure you let me know if the ice starts pressing. And call me if there's anything else that bothers you. OK?'

'Aye, aye, Skipper,' he replied.

I felt delirious just lifting my swollen ankles on to the bunk and, of course, the arms of Morpheus soon enfolded me … Then bang, clatter! What was that racket on the stairs? For a pretty calm sort of guy, Alan was certainly agitated now. 'Sorry, Skipper. But there's an iceberg steaming straight towards us.'

'*Steaming* towards us?'

'Yes, Skipper. Well, it's coming through the ice. It's making a bow wave of the floes!'

'I'll come on up.'

Back on the bridge, things appeared unchanged. Sweeping round with the bridge corner searchlight revealed the same peaceful scene – calm floes and great ice pancakes with strange ice sculptures on their rifted edges – disturbed only by one rogue iceberg. It was just two compass points off the starboard bow and was definitely pushing through the floes towards us, or so it seemed. I immediately rang stand by on the engine-room telegraph. 'OK,' I said to the mate. 'Get some men on the fore end as look-outs again. We're moving out of here. This berg is obviously aground at ninety fathoms and the current is taking us towards it. We'd better get out of its way.'

Slow speed on the engines had us pushing the ice-floes steadily clear. The fog had lifted at last and we could now see for some distance, allowing me to identify some space among the ice ahead of us, both visually and on the radar. Perhaps we could move a little more quickly if we were careful. I was now more aware than ever of the time we had lost and of the need to get on to more fish.

Taking hold of the binoculars, I decided to climb the mast to spot the best way out. The crew looked on with interest. There was still a sharp frost in the air, and after two or three minutes on top of the cross-trees I could see what direction we needed to take. Then I moved to a position on the bridge top for a more distant view, and by stationing the look-out at an open window I was able to relay my instructions to the wheelman.

'Starboard five. Amidships. Steady as she goes.'

I stayed on the bridge top throughout the morning, spurning breakfast now that we were making good progress at last. But it was icy up there and even my duffel-coat failed to stop the cold, which eventually penetrated right through to my bones. My face seemed to freeze up and I ended up talking like a ventriloquist's dummy. No one could understand a word I said. But my vigil did the trick and by the time I came down to thaw out with a bowl of soup we had clear water ahead of us.

Still, the hours I was putting in were taking their toll. Once the pressure was off, I felt very weary so I left it to the bosun to take the next watch. We steamed up towards the Hellefiske Banks, first trying the Frederikshaab Bank, where a great glacier spawned all the icebergs dotting these waters. We found fish there all right. But I was unfamiliar with the ground, and we were doing too much damage to the trawl, so I steamed further north, finally hitting heavy fishing on the Little Hellefiske Bank. My time was nearly up and I considered extending our trip by a couple of days, but it wouldn't look good on the market. And it would be a complete waste of time if the fish suddenly took off, as often happened in these circumstances.

We turned the amount of fish on board into a decent trip, certainly much better than Larsen's, and I decided to set off for home while the weather was fine, hoping to clear the ice-fields round Cape Farewell before the fog came down again. We ran quickly across the North Atlantic with a westerly gale Force Eight behind us, practically surfing down the twenty- to thirty-foot waves. I had to watch the wheelman all the time to look lively. He had to make sure we didn't broach to and get swamped. It happened on a couple of occasions and we ended up thrown on our beam ends. So yet more hours on the bridge for me.

At last we passed through the Pentland Firth, a tricky exercise with a gale up your arse. It's like rafting through white water. And then the final test, taking a ship down the Humber – never an easy river to negotiate unless you have the experience. We rounded up and were just going alongside the jetty at St Andrew's Dock, when my heart skipped a beat. Was that Janet there on the quay to meet me? Sadly no. Once again it was a girl in similar clothing. Strange how your heart takes a kick when you think you've spotted the one you love.

Greenland had been a tough test for a skipper so early in his career, and my body was now feeling the strain. Please God, I'd get more than two and a half days at home. But it wasn't to be. Although I'd done so well, I was asked to go straight back in the *Keverne* as mate with Fargy. That's what fishing was all about.

Since my time with Janet was going to be limited I decided to take the plunge. I gave her the address of the house I'd been looking at and invited her to drive over in her new car and meet me. 'I'm thinking of buying it,' I told her when she pulled up outside. 'What do you think?'

'The deposit must be huge,' she replied. 'Are you sure you can afford it?'

We went inside. Jan thought the house was beautiful. 'Do you reckon you could live somewhere like this?' I asked her.

'Could I?' she gasped. 'Just give me the chance.'

'That's exactly what I am doing. I'm asking you to marry me and live here. I'll be away for long periods, though. You might find you get lonely.'

'Not when Mum and Dad see this place. They'll love helping to set it up for us.'

'Shall we do it then?'

She looked up at me, eyes sparkling. 'Yes, please,' she said.